"Among my favourite reads of 2022. In a time of instant gratification, Julian King provides an essential reminder that our journeys and reflections upon them are where our growth and learning reside. Through a poignant and amusing individual and family story, with clean reflection points for the reader, he elegantly exposes a framework to access the most powerful learning and growth available to all of us for a better future...the successes and failures of our lived lives so far. The REALM model he unfolds has practical application in purpose, self-audit, and direction to anyone, at any stage of their journey, to create contentment in the moment and purpose for the future."

Dr Adrian Waite, Head of Talent, Boehringer-Ingelheim IMETA

"The Cowbells is a simple and lovely story told with humanity that moved me deeply. It invites the reader to ask profound questions about their own life. Julian King is a wise man, master coach, and poetic storyteller. I could not recommend a more humane coach to help anyone discover the important answers of our own big questions. The Cowbells shows Julian's luminescent wisdom in its rare glory."

Sean Blair, Founder at ProMeet and LEGO© Serious Play© Method Series Author

For Maya and Xavyn
May the road always rise to meet ye

Version 1.0

ISBN 978-1-7392550-1-5

Published by orangecairns Ltd

Cover Design @websquesuben

Table of Contents

Foreword

How can I live a full and meaningful life?

The age-old question. One that I have struggled with and one that so many of the people I coach struggle with. Some may say it's a sign of the times with world crises, the Great Resignation, priorities changing from generation to generation, and so much more, but let's face it, we've been sitting around the fire reflecting on this since, well, since we started sitting around fires.

How can I walk my own unique path?

A few years ago I realised there were a couple of elements to this question that show up repeatedly in the people I work with. The first of these themes is around self-awareness and self-leadership. So many of us think we know all the ins and outs of who we are. Then something happens which pulls the rug out from under us, and we see there are gaps as wide as mountain passes running through that knowledge.

The other area centres on clarity of direction. Call it what we will – our purpose, our way forward, our contribution, our *ikigai*, our big hairy audacious goal, or simply what gets us off the sofa every day. Typically, this presents itself through loss, maybe the loss of a role or a relationship or a loved one or our health. Sometimes this loss is of time. Something makes us realise that our stay on this blue planet is limited. It shows up as well with the achievement of a goal, be it career status, a business or project objective, financial freedom, a target hit... And of course, achievement is also a loss as we no longer have something to aim for.

On seeing this, I went on my own discovery process to dig deeper. In addition to my coaching background, I trained as a counsellor. I read a lot of books. I talked to anyone who would share their lives with me. I climbed a lot of mountains to think.

Out of all this came a focussed approach to help people better explore themselves and their way forward. Like many, I'm wary of models and the associated simplification, yet this one seems to work. And out of this structure – chicken or egg - came this story as a way of bringing it to life. For we have also always told stories since we started sitting around fires.

Enjoy the book and the questions and the journey.

Most importantly, be well.

Julian, December 2022

Prologue

"Tell me, what is it you plan to do with your one wild and precious life?"
Mary Oliver

Silvia Climbs A Mountain

The day Silvia learned she was going to die was one like many others in western Scotland. There'd been sun and rain and mist and cloud, and now the weather gods were debating throwing in hail and snow as well. Halfway up Ben More on the Isle of Mull, the wettest of the Hebrides, Silvia felt one or both would be fitting on such a late autumn day. Some thunder and lightning wouldn't go amiss either if the gods were doing the dramatic, why not.

When the message came through on her phone, she sat down on a rock by the side of the path and had a bit of a cry. After a while, she realised she was crying for herself and felt guilty, so she switched to crying for her family, and then in time for her friends too. Once she got to people like Laura and Carmen who she hadn't seen since school years ago and couldn't even remember their faces now come to think of it, she considered she was probably pushing it, and so she stopped and simply looked out to sea. She'd never been much good at self-pity. A passing couple in their sixties paused by her.

"You alright there?", the man asked softly. The kindness of strangers. Silvia smiled weakly and nodded.

"It's not that bad of a climb," the woman offered gently to cheer her up.

Silvia laughed more than the joke deserved, in gratitude if nothing else. "Just a little further, eh?"

"That's the spirit." The couple beamed at her, nodded goodbye as one, and carried on upwards hand in hand.

Silvia watched them go. In her mid-fifties, she was not going to make their age. The tears threatened to return, and so she cast her eyes back out to sea again. The waters were choppy and grey, with white caps racing by. Not the kind of sea in which it'd be easy to spot whales or dolphins, too rough even for the Staffa sightseeing boats. The wind picked up stronger, and she huddled into herself.

Stage four breast cancer. Well, that was a bit of a bitch, all in all. They'd thought it was gone, zapped and chemoed out of her system, yet here it was, back and on a mission too. This Christmas would be her last, if she made it that far. Her birthday in February? Not a chance, apparently.

She'd known the news was due today, good or bad. Needing space for herself, she'd rented a cottage on Mull for a few days, packed the car up in Edinburgh, and crossed over on the last ferry from Oban yesterday. Only her girlfriend knew what was going on. Jacqui'd been surprised and for sure, hurt to feel excluded like this, but she'd had the grace to not insist. If this was what Silvia wanted, Jacqui knew there wasn't much point arguing.

It's said that when our lives are turned upside down in a less than great way, we dip and plunge in and out of anger, denial, depression, bargaining and acceptance in broken loops and spirals and sudden leaps. Silvia, being a practical sort, rushed through all five before hitting on the nature of her own death as being a useful distraction from the eddies.

And so she sat on her rock and did her usual rationalising thing. She had a habit of thinking in bullet points, which infuriated most of her family, but she's just had bad news so let's not be too harsh. Silvia reasoned how our lives are never the same after that day in childhood when we somehow discover:

- That everything and everyone dies.
- That not only is it going to happen to all of us at some point, but also, try what you may, there's no getting away from it.
- And that when it does happen, that's it, there's no coming back. Even Count Dracula dies eventually.

This is one cold, hard truth that most of us find a little too cold and a little too hard. So, sensibly or not, she reflected, we then park this truth away at the back of our minds and go off and do something less uncomfortable. Every now and then the pesky little meerkat will pop its head back up to remind us *Hey, I'm still here*, but by and large we get on with everything. It's what we do.

Squinting into the swirling wind, Silvia pulled a lock of hair out of her eye. At school, they'd only just stopped calling her the Mad Hatter. Better than the Crazy Baldhead she'd got at home all the way through her chemo. The thought brought a smile at the irreverent love she enjoyed. Cheered, she returned to her deduction.

So when the Grim Reaper does inevitably enter stage left, she continued to muse, it shouldn't really be such a shock, should it? Of course, he - definitely a he, she decided - takes some of us so abruptly we don't get the chance to be surprised. In our sleep, in an explosion, in a car crash, in a rifle shot, in an aneurysm. Here one moment, toast the next.

For others, death lingers in the shadows, weaving a gradual decline after a life long lived. There's a vague awareness, a darkening as the senses draw in, a candle tapering before finally flickering out. Even then you don't really have to confront it. It just kinda happens...

And then there's the death which rudely walks into your house without knocking or asking to be let in. The death which sits there in your favourite chair in the drawing room wondering if you'd like a game of chess to pass the time while you try and get your head round your options. Before you know it, this death has whipped out his chess clock timer and gleefully slammed it tick-tocking away between you. Four minutes. A week. Three months. Tomorrow at dawn...

She'd been given Option Three. At least there was that clarity. Still, Silvia wished there was an old mystic in a cave on the mountain so she could go and sit at their feet and have a really good and lengthy chinwag about it all. Alcohol or at the very least a big pot of tea would need to be involved. Silvia felt some enlightenment would go a long way to balancing her day out.

Her thoughts came back to the others. Jacqui. Her three children. Her ex-husband. Her brother. Her mother over in Chile. What was she going to do about them? Silvia worked her way through the hows and what ifs with each of her loved ones. She wondered what lives they would lead, where they would go, who they would meet. Would her daughter Gabriella make it as an actor as she dreamed? Would her ex ever write his book? Would David skip the awkward beard stage? How could she help them all?

A group of young teenagers passed by on their way down the mountain, chattering among themselves and barely giving her a look.

Silvia hoped she was different at their age but doubted it. She'd rushed through everything too, constantly surprised at wherever she turned up.

Silvia had now spent an hour sitting on the rock. She was giving it far more warmth than she was getting back, so she stretched her legs out and carefully got to her feet. She looked at the views all around her. An hour lost in her thoughts on a cold, grey mountain far from home. She was going to have to go back to Edinburgh and tell them. Her mind went to how each would take the news.

Yet more than this, she realised something else weighed on her. She loved them all, but she could see there were rough edges. Silvia had never considered people as jigsaws, as either complete or with pieces missing, and she certainly wasn't going to start now. In her eyes, we constantly grow and veer off in often unexpected directions. A bit like plants or rivers or even this mountain path.

However, there were undeniably a few little things that would help her loved ones all live better. She was far from perfect, but she'd thought she'd be around to share their journeys and guide where she could. Again, she teared up.

"Enough," she said out aloud to herself. Enough with the maudlin and with the gloom. She'd head back east tomorrow, and deal with it all. But right here, right now, there was a mountain to climb. And there might even be an old mystic somewhere up there with a bottle of whisky and a tale to tell. That'd be worth fighting a little longer for. And so she walked on.

Self-Reflection

1. What kind of a person do you think Silvia is?
2. How have you experienced the 'kindness of strangers'?
3. How did you learn about death in your childhood?
4. What image or metaphor would you use to describe your life so far?

Part One

"Listen. Make a way for yourself inside yourself. Stop looking in the other way of looking. You already have the precious mixture that will make you well. Use it."

Rumi

1. Henry Sets The Scene

From his seat on the red beanbag, Henry Maclean quietly studies the faces in the room. 63, bald, and with his beanbag-sitting days sadly long behind him, he's been practising law in his beloved Edinburgh for decades. Admittedly a little old-fashioned in his ways for some, he prides himself on the care and attention he puts into his work. He likes to think he's developed over the years just the right blend of compassion and authority in his diction and tone for times like these. Yet the solicitor suspects today is high if not top on the list of unusual will readings he's had to give in his career.

As if picking up on his mood, the six people in the school room with him shift in their own beanbags drawn up in a circle. It's a Saturday afternoon and the school is empty except for the young caretaker who hovers in the corridor outside pretending to be busy with a fusebox.

In the centre of the ring stand seven worn cowbells of different sizes and colours. There's a rumble of impatience from one of the men on his right - the brother, Henry seems to recollect. The man awkwardly rolls himself onto his feet, takes off his coat, and goes to hang it on a hook on the wall before sitting back down. A crayon drawing of a lion is stuck to the wall just next to the coat in a way Henry finds oddly appropriate. He rubs his glasses with his tie and puts them back on. "Ladies and gentlemen," he begins before giving the room a moment to settle. "Ladies and gentlemen," he repeats, "this is the last will and testament of Silvia Elena Vazquez, late of 44 Craigmonth Avenue, Edinburgh. Ms Vazquez…Silvia was explicit in her wishes for you to hear these particular terms together as a group. Indeed as a family even. The choice of her own schoolroom where she taught for many years as the setting for this is, in my humble view, as wonderfully unique as the person I found Silvia to be." Henry's pleased to note the nervous smiles and shared glances between his listeners.

"The financial aspects of her estate will be discussed with each of you individually and privately following this meeting. Suffice to say at this stage that in a very broad manner of speaking, this estate has been equally divided between you. As such, the terms today consist of a series of…tasks she has designed specifically for each of you. She was also adamant that any financial endowments were dependent in each case on the tasks being fully completed to my satisfaction."

Henry pauses to let the import of his words sink in. He takes a sip of water from his glass and once more scans the faces. The man he'd rightly taken to be the brother grins back at him. "Good ol' sis. I knew she'd have some fun with us." His mood lightens the tension in the room and it seems as if the others all breathe out at once.

The elder of the two sons, Mauricio if Henry remembers correctly, harrumphs. "Well, let's see what she's got in store for us first." The younger woman, Gabriella as Henry surreptitiously checks in his notes, turns to give her brother a scowl worthy of a kabuki performance to put him in his place.

Henry knows not to keep the suspense burning any longer. "So…", he picks up a sheet of paper from in front of him and holds it to the light. Although it's only mid-afternoon, the world outside is already darkening with the February twilight. "In her words as she wished...*My dear loved ones. My beautiful children, Mauricio, Gabriella, and David. My bestest brother Ignacio. My fantastic Kieran. My gorgeous Jacqui. Along with my mother in Chile you are all I have loved and love still, wherever I am now.*" Henry looks over the top of the sheet of paper at them, smiles gently, and drops his eyes again. "*Thanks to you I have lived well, if not as long as I'd expected. I trust you don't hold it against me for going too soon. I wanted to go out on my terms, not on those of this vile disease. Anyway, you know how I am with love and how important it is to me. I had hoped to see you all embraced in love in time. My children and my baby brother with whoever deserved you, my Kieran with whoever would care for you as much as I have done. And for you, my dearest Jacqui, I had a bag of ruses to convince you to limbo down the aisle one day...*"

There's a sob from Jacqui and she lifts her hand in apology. Sitting beside her, Kieran reaches over to lay a hand on her shoulder. He softly nods at the solicitor to continue.

Henry clears his throat. "*I think as human beings it is only when we are in loving relationships that we are full. And you have made me so very full over my life. But I cannot command you to be in love or even to find love. It will come to you when you are ready. Yet there is something you can do for me. Something you can do for yourselves and for all of us. You can lead lives full of meaning, full of purpose, full of direction. You can live well. If I think of you now as I write these words, I am sorry to say you are not doing this. It pains me to leave you like this. And so, please don't be angry with me, you know I'm batshit loca* – I hope I pronounced that correctly," interjects Henry before continuing. *"I have prepared individual tasks for all six of you to do. In a year's time, when you have accomplished each of them, you are to meet again as a group with Henry and to report back on what you have learnt. Only when Henry is satisfied that you have achieved the objective of the task will he discuss the financial terms with you. Henry will give you your tasks now. He will also give you a cowbell to ring when you have achieved your task. For a bit of fun, like life itself. My darlings, enjoy the tasks and live well. You will see what I mean soon enough. I love you all. More than I could ever hope to express, I love you. Now, as our Costa Rican friends say, pura vida! Live well."*

Henry puts the sheet of paper down in his lap and waits for everyone to compose themselves. After a moment he reaches for the brown A4 envelope in front of him and slices it open with a letter knife. He empties out six white cards onto the carpet and sorts them into order. He picks up the top one and turns to the youngest son, a man in his early twenties.

"David, this one's for you. On one side there's a sentence, which you're to read out to everyone. On the other side are the instructions for your task, which you're to keep to yourself until we meet again as a group. Here you go." Henry hands over the card.

Wide-eyed with all that is happening, David takes the card. It has a pencil sketch of a tree with long roots, under which a sentence is written in bold. He reads this sentence to himself and then immediately flips the card over to read the task. He gulps as he does so and his eyes well up.

Across from him, his father Kieran gently asks after a moment, "What does your sentence say, son?"

David looks up at him, lost and overwhelmed. And then finally, "I am rooted."

His father smiles at him and nods encouragingly.

Henry adds, "Good. Now take any one of the cowbells."

David scans the seven before opting for the most battered looking. It gives a dull thunk as he puts it in his lap. He smiles shyly at the group.

Henry selects another card and holds it out to the daughter. "And this one's for you, Gabriella."

Gabriella takes it and reads out, "I am excellent." She looks round the circle, admires the picture of a gold star on the card, and then turns it over to read the other side. She lets out a soft whistle, almost like her younger brother, but does not say anything else. After a moment she remembers and reaches out to take a rusty gold-coloured cowbell. She puts it down beside her and goes back to her thoughts.

Henry holds a card out to Kieran, who says, "Thanks. It reads, I am authentic." He scans the instructions on the other side, exhales, and tucks the card into his jacket pocket. "No pressure at all," he jokes, making a silent scream. "The picture's of a heart, by the way," he adds. He chooses a heavy black cowbell and playfully strains to drag it across the floor to his side.

Henry looks at Jacqui and offers her the fourth card. The image on it is of a passport. Barely audible, Jacqui breathes, "I am loose." She reads the other side to herself but does not raise her eyes to meet the others'. She quietly selects a small silver bell and places it in her lap.

Henry takes the fifth card and leans over to hand it to Ignacio, who beams at them all. "What a woman she was, my big sister…" He looks down at the card. "I have a mission." He turns it over and his face clouds as he reads the other side to himself. Between his fingers, the others catch the picture of a compass drawn on the card. A single tear rolls down his cheek. He stretches over to take a tall bell made of bronze.

The others turn to Mauricio, who has already grabbed the last card. He reads it all in silence, before folding the card up and shoving it in his pocket. He reaches forward and triumphantly takes the shinier of the two remaining cowbells. When he catches them all looking at him expectantly, he blurts out, "I have momentum. And it's got some hands on it. Happy?" Gabriella rolls her eyes and turns back to the solicitor.

Henry waits for a moment, and then, "Good. You all have your cards and your instructions. If there are any questions or you need any support, you are to approach me and me alone. Here is my business card for each of you. I look forward to seeing you all again, 3pm, 26th February next year, at a location to be announced beforehand. Enjoy your tasks and good luck!"

And with that, Henry painfully gets to his feet and collects his things. He stops to consider the last cowbell standing on its own in the middle. With a faint smile, he picks the dull, grey bell up, gives them all a final nod, and leaves the room.

Self-Reflection
1. What kind of a family do you think Silvia's is?
2. How would you feel if a loved one set you tasks to do from beyond the grave?
3. Which of the six sentences on the cards are you the most curious about?
4. What could be the role of the cowbells?

2. David Goes On A Journey

The plane banks, bringing the long line of the Andes clearly into view through the left-side windows. David tightens his seatbelt as the plane levels out again and then suddenly dips down sharply through a layer of cloud towards Santiago. David looks out at the city sitting in its huge bowl, the mountains rising steeply to cut off any further expansion.

This is a day of firsts. His first trip alone since Covid. His first time south of the equator. And most importantly, his first visit to Chile, the country where his mother was born. And yet he isn't sure if they truly are firsts. He isn't really alone for a start. His mother is with him in a small box in his suitcase. He hadn't been too sure what the rules were for carrying ashes across international boundaries, and so Mum's in a very unflattering Tupperware box for the time being. She'd always had stories about travelling cheaply in hostels and camping out in the wild before she had a family, so he feels she wouldn't mind her temporary accommodation too much.

And that's the other thing. She'd also always had all these wonderful tales about her early childhood in Chile. The sights, the smells, the tastes, the songs, the people she missed so much in distant Edinburgh. In a way it's like he's already been here.

The man in the seat next to him catches his eager look. "*Bienvenido a Chile,*" he smiles. "Welcome."

"*Gracias,*" replies David politely. He grips the seat as the plane hits an air pocket.

The man smiles again. "It's always a shade rough coming in." His tone is American but David can hear the Chilean behind. This seems to him more reassuring than the words.

It's the Easter break and David is taking his mother home, as his card had instructed. The idea is that he will finish off his degree remotely at his grandmother's place. He just has a few exams left, everything else is done. The summer term and then the summer holidays in Chile. Well, the UK summer at least. South of the equator it's all upside down. Or maybe it's vice versa, as his mother always used to point out.

His grandmother lives on the island of Chiloé, far to the south of Santiago. Her town is called Quellón, and it's literally the end of the road. The end of the Panamerican Highway at least. David has no idea what to expect when he gets there, but it's certainly going to be an experience.

"Come here. You're too British."

The arms of David's grandmother loom wide. With a sheepish smile, David lets himself be taken into them and hugged till he's breathless. It's been a few years since Guillermina last visited them in Edinburgh, and there are a lot of hugs to catch up on.

She comes from the classic grandmother mould – four feet tall and wide, white hair rising untamed in all directions, not a care in the world for what anyone thinks of her. A ball of love and fire too. Guillermina points at his bag, "Is she…?"

David nods softly.

His grandmother smiles, "Good, my daughter's home again." She winks at David, "Your home too… Not that you know anything about it, do you? Anthropology student, a year in Japan, trips here and there, but no idea about your own background."

David knows better than to be baited. He looks at her wooden house up on its stilts and the early morning mist still hanging over the land. It'd been a long bus ride down overnight from Santiago. "I know you're a *machi*, a shaman," he can't resist.

"We prefer healer," his grandmother scowls, but as she steps aside to let him in, he catches her grinning.

"So, young man, what are you going to do?"

Later the same day, they're sitting out on his grandmother's terrace at the back, the twilight darkening around them. David looks at the snow on the mountain peaks still lit up on the mainland in the distance. Closer by, fishing boats bob in the water. He still can't get his head around the fact he is finally in Chile after all these years. He sighs, "That's the question. I don't really know."

Guillermina takes a sip of her red wine and leans back in her chair. "Your grandfather did anthropology. Look where it got him," she cackles, more to herself than to her grandson.

"Everyone else at uni just seems so much more...sussed with everything. Career plans, where they want to live, how many kids they're going to have, all that..." David drifts off before downing the rest of his wine in a gulp and reaching for the bottle.

Guillermina studies him over her glass. She hadn't known him to be so indecisive and lost before. As the youngest of her three grandchildren, he's the one she's spent the least time with. As soon as Pinochet died in 2006, she'd got on a plane and returned to Chile from her exile in Scotland. Silvia and Ignacio had made their separate lives in Edinburgh, and so they stayed on. David had only been six when she left. And yet this earnest child of a man is the one Guillermina loves most. She can't quite put her finger on why. Guillermina carefully gets to her feet and leans on the railing around the edge of the terrace. If people are either water or mountain, she is definitely the former. She eyes the sea and all its movements. "It might seem strange to you how looking back can be the best way to move forward."

David looks up at her expectantly, waiting for her to continue.

"If you know where you come from. Your story. Your values. What you stand for. What has got you to this place on the map. If you have all that, then you can chart your way forward from this point on the road. Seem true?", she watches him out of the corner of her eye.

David shrugs. "Seems true," he offers, uncommitted.

Guillermina turns to face him full on. "Right, so if we're going to respect your mother's wishes, you're going to have to learn about your grandfather and our people, the Huilliche..."

"I thought we had Mapuche origins," interrupts David.

"Huilliche means people of the south. We're a branch of the Mapuche," continues his grandmother, shaking her head. "Here on Chiloé, most of our indigenous people are Cunco, but we're Huilliche. So much you don't know. There's a museum in town where you should start. *Inchin Cuivi Anti*. It means 'our ancestors'. Our ancestors lived on this land. We honour them by keeping their stories alive. That will be part of looking at who you really are. But first of all, even before our own language Huilliche, we need to polish up your Spanish. From now on, no more English."

"But..."

"*Ya basta, solo español!*"

David looks round the classroom a little sceptically. There are only seven other students milling around, all hovering by a table where there are coffee cups and some plates of biscuits. Listening in to the various introductions and conversations going on, he learns his colleagues are a mixture of ages and nationalities. A pair of Canadian yoga instructors in their late 20s, an Arab couple in their forties or so, a German aid worker, an American retiree, and a Chinese businessman of some kind.

A woman more or less his age comes in with a large flask of coffee, which she hands to David with a smile before going to open one of the curtains wider. He stands there nonplussed for a moment until he realises she wants him to fill the cups. As he does so, the woman calls out, "*Gracias.*"

David replies automatically, "You're welcome."

"*De nada*," the woman corrects him.

Ah, the teacher. David bows his head apologetically, and is rewarded with another smile. He has a feeling he might enjoy this class after all.

At barely 20,000 inhabitants, it has to be said Quellón isn't a huge place, but it still manages to pack in quite a few bars. It's the end of the first week of the intensive Spanish course and the class are all having a drink together with their teacher Montse down in the port area. David's pleased to see his Spanish is freer again after a few years of hardly speaking it at all. His mother had always insisted that her children were bilingual, which was useful towards the end when the drugs she was taking for the cancer affected her more and more. Silvia had often lapsed into her native tongue in her semi-conscious ramblings. The memory leaves a cloud on David's face.

Catching his mood, Montse leans over to distract him, "For someone who's never been to Chile before, your Chilean accent's quite good."

"And for a Catalan – Montse's a Catalan name, isn't it? – your Chilean isn't too bad either," replies David with a smile.

"Good call," she clinks her glass of beer with his.

"My Catalan friends in Edinburgh would struggle with the concept of one of their own teaching Spanish," adds David thoughtfully.

"Yes, well, needs must. It pays for me to stay here while I do my research," offers Montse levelly.

"Your research?"

"Spanish colonialism, broadly, but please, not tonight. It's too heavy. Fancy another?", she asks.

"Sure, let me help you," he replies and they both walk up to the bar together. As they get there, their German colleague comes out of the bathroom and accidentally knocks into one of a pair of guys drinking heavily at the other end of the bar. The German is apologetic but the man stands up and starts shouting at him drunkenly. At once David goes over and stands between them. He motions for the German to go and sit down before working to appease the drunken man. After a few minutes, he and the man are the best of friends and calm has been restored. David pats him on the shoulder and comes back to rejoin his teacher.

Montse nods, impressed. "You handled that well."

"I've worked in a few pubs to pay my way through university. You should see a Hibs-Hearts derby."

"Hibs? Hearts?," asks Montse confused.

"Football."

"Ah," nods Montse. "What did you say to him?"

"Well, he was calling me a *gringo* till I pointed out who my grandmother was. That seemed to work. Poor guy lost a pal at sea off his boat this week. It's amazing how few fishermen around the world can actually swim," David shakes his head. He leans on the bar, and then more reflectively adds, "The Japanese have a saying for it. *The surface may be calm, but underneath the keel everything is chaos.* The guy there made me think of that all of a sudden."

"So which are you, Chilean or *gringo*?," asks Montse, looking at him straight.

David smiles, "That's what I'm here to find out, I guess."

"What should I call you?," asks Montse as she looks up from the garden to where David's grandmother is standing in her front door.

"Guillermina, like in the Neruda poem," she winks at David.

David guffaws, "Would he have been another of your 'friends', *Abuela*? My gran has had a number of friends throughout her life," he explains to Montse.

"I can imagine," says Montse approvingly.

"I like her already. Come on in, both of you," replies Guillermina, stepping aside to let them pass.

It's several weeks later, and David has thought it only right to introduce the two women between who he spends his time. Guillermina has chosen to celebrate the occasion with a lunch of traditional curanto stew, full of shellfish, beef, potatoes and more. As they sit down, she says, "I may indeed have known a few people along the way, but this I keep for my special people." She smiles at them both and then adds quietly, "It was the favourite of David's grandfather."

Montse instinctively reaches a hand out to the old woman's. "Tell us about him."

"Well," starts Guillermina more lightly again. "He had his moments. He was no angel. Always fighting this or fighting that. He had a strong sense of justice, what was right and wrong. Just like David... But he was also very romantic. Maybe like David too, no?"

David can't help blushing as the two women look at him, each with love. Embarrassed, he moves the conversation on, "He was half Scots, half Huilliche, wasn't he?"

Guillermina nods, "His own father was from a tiny place on the Argyll coast. We went there once but you'd have been too young to remember."

Montse jokes, "He must have felt right at home here with all the rain."

Guillermina nods, "*Como no*, of course. My husband always said he was a hard man, but fair.... He was a strong influence on your mother, you know," she says looking at David for a moment. And then, "Come, you're not eating. It'll get cold," she admonishes the two youngsters.

Montse dutifully takes a spoonful before asking, "How did you find Scotland?"

Guillermina brightens. "Oh, a beautiful place. Beautiful. But not mine. My place is here. These are my people. We had to leave when Pinochet... My husband was a university professor and also an activist for our people. His type didn't last long after the coup happened. The

27

last time I saw him he had a meeting with some other professors he was going to... He never got there... Some friends came round later that night. Said it wasn't safe for us to stay, so through one family to another, I made my way out with Silvia and Ignacio. They were just children. It was a hard decision, but I felt, how can we say, that I owed them a future. We went to Barcelona first, and then eventually to Scotland. A very kind lawyer helped us get refugee status... But no, lovely as it was, it wasn't my country. I couldn't wait to get back."

His eyes glistening, David puts his hand on her arm, "You did your bit. Mum was always talking about you going off and getting arrested on some protest or another. Like that time Pinochet was in England and you headed south on the bus to demonstrate. She said it was a miracle we weren't all deported."

The mood lightens as Guillermina grins. And then in a beat she's serious again. "My husband was always curious about people. He said if you're curious about something, you can't be afraid of it. You can only want good. And that too, I think David has, don't you?" She turns to the young woman.

Now it's Montse's turn to blush as she looks from one to the other. She nods, not trusting herself to speak.

As if satisfied, Guillermina asks, "Good, enough of the past for the time being. What are you *jóvenes* going to do now that the course has finished?"

David, looking at Montse, answers, "We thought we'd explore the mainland, maybe go north to Atacama for a bit. Take a bus up and see the desert after all this wet. Maybe go and see some Mapuche communities in the south too."

Guillermina beams at them both. "That sounds like a very sensible idea indeed. But no bus. I have a surprise for you. Come with me." And with that she takes them both by the hand and leads them out of the house and around to the garage at the side. With some difficulty, she manages to unlock the two wooden doors and then pull them both back. Inside there's a gorgeous old tan Cadillac with whitewall tyres and a hardtop, all gleaming as if new.

"It's a 1971 Coupe DeVille," says Guillermina proudly, basking in their wonder. "It was your grandfather's pride and joy."

David can't resist getting in and turning the engine on. It springs to life with a stutter and a cough and then more fully. "How...?" Guillermina brushes the question away, "Oh, a friend comes by every now and then to play with it." There's an undeniable sparkle in her eye.

David gets out of the car and comes over to give her a big hug. Guillermina motions at Montse, "Come here, you too."

After a long moment she pulls away from them both. "Now, go and explore, David. And when you're ready, come back and tell me what you've found about yourself. And you, my dear, don't let him come back till he knows his roots."

David and Montse both nod solemnly. And then they turn to look at each other and can't help giggling with excitement.

Self-Reflection

1. What do you think about the idea of looking back to look forward?
2. What influences have played out so far on David's life?
3. What are the childhood influences that you still carry with you?
4. Which values have led you to live as you do?

3. Gabriella Acts Up

Gabriella rolls over in her bed and hits the snooze button on the alarm clock. She looks over at the cot but miraculously her daughter Harmony is still asleep. She hears her father shout something up at her about breakfast and then there's the sound of the front door closing. Silence and freedom.

Gabriella stretches under the covers and runs through her opening lines one more time. The dress rehearsal for the play is in two days and she's starting to freak, truth be told. It's only an amateur production, but she's felt like an open wound ever since Mum died. The slightest thing sends her off on a crying jag. She wonders how everyone else seems to keep it so together. And then there's the card and all that pressure. *Get into drama school and get great.* Oh yes and, *I am excellent.* That's it. Batshit *loca* doesn't come close, she thinks gently and then wells up.

To take her mind off things, she focusses in again. *"Ismene, dear sister, / You would think that we had already suffered enough / For the curse on Oedipus: / I cannot imagine any grief / That you and I have not gone through. And now - / Have they told you of the new decree of our King Creon?"*

Antigone. It's a meaty role, an important role, a role that talks to her and her belief in standing up for yourself. She's proud of herself for getting the part. Becca and Teri had gone for it too. She hopes their friendship will spark again once the show's over. For the last few weeks it's been all little looks and comments between themselves whenever she walks by, tumbleweeds when she posts anything. So be it.

There's supposed to be a technical run through that afternoon, but Gabriella's already arranged to meet Martin in town. Someone else can stand in for her. Right now though, it's time for a shower. She wonders if Martin will like her new perfume. If he even notices, she frowns. He calls her his Girl From Ipanema, which is frankly strange as no one in her family has been near Brazil to her knowledge. Anyway, she's sure he has his good points.

She'll go over her lines again tonight if she has time.

The rehearsal is a shocker. Gabriella repeatedly forgets her lines to the point where Simon, the director, brings his copy of the play over for her to hold in her hand. She thinks she sees Becca and Teri giggling to each other in the wings. That's when she really loses the plot. Literally. They'd changed some of the stage positioning around during the run through which she'd missed. The lighting director keeps having to look for her with the spotlight.

At the end, there's a long moment of silence and then the rest of the cast drift backstage to the dressing rooms. Everyone carefully avoids looking Gabriella in the eye.

Simon calls her over to where he sits halfway up the hall with the producer, Sophie, a rake-thin woman in her forties with a cigarette always lodged between her fingers. "That was fucking awful, Gabi," he says as she walks up. "Do you even know the lines?"

Simon's a few years younger than her and not the most reliable of guys himself, but Gabriella knows she's in the wrong. She looks at the floor, not daring to speak.

"Teri's all over the part. She's ready to step in if need be," continues Simon. "What do you think?" He turns to Sophie for support but she ignores him, studying Gabriella.

Softly, she offers, "You've got this, haven't you, Gabriella?"

Gabriella can't help a quickly muffled sob, but she nods once and then more firmly twice. "I've got this," she breathes in no more than a whisper.

Simon looks from one to the other, more in disbelief than irritation, and shakes his head. After a moment, "Don't make me regret this, Gabi. The play's got more riding on it than just your ego. We're on tomorrow." The chair seat slams back as he jumps to his feet and strides off.

Once he's left the hall, Gabriella looks down at her mentor, "Thank you."

Sophie leans back in her seat and eyes her straight. "You're a good actor, Gabriella, but you don't put the work in. You think it'll all come to you. Out there, what just happened, that was embarrassing. I'd say you were just going through the motions but even that would be too generous. You're wasting everyone's time and you're wasting your own. We don't get too many chances in this line of work." She stands up and wraps herself in her coat.

And with that, Sophie looks at her watch, grins at Gabriella mischievously, "Bollocks, late again," and shoots off herself, coat and scarf flying along behind her. Gabriella stands all on her own and gulps back the tears.

"What's up, sweetheart?", asks Kieran as his daughter absent-mindedly drifts a fork around and through and across the pasta he's so proudly cooked. He hopes his voice doesn't carry any of the mild frustration he's feeling at the lack of appreciation for his newfound cooking prowess.

Gabriella looks up at her father and out of nowhere the floodgates open. *Whoa*, thinks Kieran as a number of questions run through his brain. All the way from *How does she do that? How can she go from Sahara to Niagara Falls at a switch?* via *Why didn't Silvia warn me about this?* and through to *What's up with my beautiful daughter? Why is she in so much pain?* He reaches over and grabs a flailing hand.

"It's the play," wails Gabriella. "I'm so crap at my lines and everything. I'm 28 and I'm a single mum and I'm living back at home and...I'm going to let everyone down, just like Sophie warned me."

Kieran comes round the table to sit beside her as she goes on, "Martin says I shouldn't worry, it's just a community theatre play, but I enjoy it and I'm good at it..." Gabriella nods her thanks at the tissue her Dad is holding out for her.

Fighting back the urge to ask who Martin is, Kieran takes her into his arms until she calms down, and then gently asks, "What would your Mum do?" It has become their little mantra together. God knows Gabriella and her mother had had some amazing rows and tantrums over the years, but there had always been a strong love.

Gabriella looks up wide-eyed at her father, and thinks for a moment. "She'd have told me to prioritise." As if on cue, there's the sound of a car horn outside. Kieran walks to the window. A black Porsche is idling in the road.

"That'll be Martin," says Gabriella, rolling her eyes in apology.

"He can't be bothered to park and come to the door to pick you up?", queries Kieran. He isn't as good an actor as his daughter. It's very clear what he thinks.

Gabriella stands up. "I'll get rid of him. Say Harmony's sick or something."

"You could just tell him the truth too," says her father.

Gabriella nods quietly. "Where are you off to?"

"To see if I've got a shotgun somewhere," mutters Kieran. Gabriella punches him on the arm and giggles.

"That's better," smiles Kieran. "When you've dispatched yon knave, do you fancy running through your lines together?"

Gabriella beams.

Gabriella smiles shyly at the attention she's getting as she wheels Harmony through the playground. Last night's opening had gone fantastically well, better than she could have dreamed. There'd been a standing ovation, flowers, and loads of people coming up to say how great she was. There was even a small piece in the local newspaper this morning with her photograph. Afterwards, her father had taken the whole family out for a meal to celebrate. Even Mauricio had been almost kind with his praise. She couldn't wait to call David in Chile about it all later.

Out of the corner of her eye, Gabriella sees Teri and Becca approaching her. She can't help stiffening a little. The two women stop right in front of her, blocking her way.

Slightly taller, Teri looks down at Gabriella. She eyes her up and down and then turns to Becca. "What do we think then?", she asks in a flat tone.

Becca follows suit in scanning Gabriella from head to toe and back again, before shrugging, "Dunno. OK, I guess?"

Teri looks from Becca back to Gabriella. "Yeah, that's what I was thinking too. OK...but maybe also just a bit bloody brilliant," and she smiles. Impulsively, Gabriella reaches out and gives her a big hug. "Hey G, steady on, no waterworks. This mascara ain't cheap." But she carries on hugging Gabriella back.

After a while, with promises to meet up for a coffee some time over the weekend, Teri and Becca hurry off to their jobs in town. Gabriella watches them go. The latest in her long line of temp jobs had finished two weeks ago. By mutual consent, she'd stressed at the dinner table that night. She looks down at her daughter calmly watching her from the pram. "I'm going to be not only the best mum you'll ever know but the best actor too. What do you think about that?", she announces.

Harmony gurgles her approval.

Gabriella rushes into the café, conscious she's nearly half an hour late. Sophie looks over at her from a table in the corner. "The star of the show," she exclaims. It isn't too clear whether this is a positive or a negative. She pulls her chair back as Gabriella settles in with a flurry of apologies. The mentor fixes her mentee with a steely gaze. "You were good last night, no doubt about that. You can act when you want to. But is that it? There are ten thousand people out there trying to get into drama school and they're all just as good as you. What's different about you? What are you going to do to be special?"

Gabriella sits in her seat and thinks. She waves away the waitress with the briefest of smiles.

Sophie eyes her unlit cigarette with evident desire. "In my day," she continues. "We had to do everything. Sing, speak French, ride a horse, play the banjo, do accents, pole-dance, anything and everything..."

She drags her chair back up close to the table, and reaches into her bag for a business card. "Maybe you could start here." She slides the card across the tabletop.

Gabriella picks the card up. "Sandy Stone. Singing Tutor to the Stars," she reads aloud. She looks at Sophie quizzically.

"Can't act to save his life, but boy can he sing. And he ain't too hard on the eyes either," Sophie grins. Her face straightens and she's all business once more. "Look, sweetheart. You've got your drama school audition in a month. A bit of singing, especially the breathing part, won't hurt. But you've got to put the work in. Right now, I'm not seeing that." She studies Gabriella to see how this lands. After a long beat, she stands up, "Anyway, you ponder about it while I go and have a ciggy." And she disappears to hover outside the front door in a cloud of smoke, oblivious to the glares from customers trying to get in or out.

In her absence, Gabriella thinks to herself, *Wow, tough crowd.* And then she wonders, *What would Mum do?*

Self-Reflection
1. What do you think of Sophie's style of feedback?
2. Do you have a Sophie in your life? What role do they play for you?
3. What are you great at?
4. How could you be even better at it?

4. Kieran Looks At Himself

Kieran sits at his desk and calmly considers how he would kill his family. He soon sees it involves more planning than might be imagined from the films. Tools, timing, sequence (Ignacio first?), location, protective clothing, pre- and post-cleaning, alibis... The list is a long one. He thinks about devising a spreadsheet but quickly realises it's all getting too Cluedo - *Mauricio with the frying pan in the kitchen* and so on. And once he gets beyond the factual to the individual human element, then it immediately starts to seep into reality. He doesn't think he could face Gabriella across an open muesli box with an easy conscience. No, a murder mystery is not for him. Ian Rankin and Denise Mina can stop looking over their shoulders.

So, if it isn't going to be death and skulduggery, what's it going to be? As Edwyn Collins has it, the possibilities are endless. As so often before, Kieran falls into all the various options and styles and genres. He knows he has a story in him, several in fact. Which would be true to him? Like a diver in tropical water, Kieran swims through his mind until a truck passing on the cobblestones outside brings him back to the present with a jump. He frowns at his laptop and throws back the last of what is now a very cold black coffee.

Still, it's been fun to be in another world for a while, a world where time seems to flow by without any due consideration for the practicalities of life. The kind of practicalities which now tell him he's going to be late for his 9 am with a small data company over on the outskirts of Craigmillar. He closes the laptop screen on yet another empty white document and heads for the door, shouting up at his daughter about breakfast as he goes. *Gabriella in the bedroom with the curling tongs* is probably the only option in her case, he reflects to himself as the front door closes behind him.

On the outskirts of Edinburgh, Craigmillar has been called an insult to humanity. Kieran wouldn't have gone so far in his appraisal – CFOs have to be circumspect in their language – but he does still pull his collar up against the cold as he looks around. Sweet wrappers and bits of newspaper dance and jig in the wind swirling around him. Inside the company and abandoned by the bored receptionist, he surveys the open plan office. He's here today to look into the books, ask a few questions, and generally see if they're worth buying. Kicking the tyres, as his boss calls it. It's not really due diligence – that would come later – but more to get a feel for them. As he waits for the managing director to appear, he wonders what the mood will be. It can be anywhere on the spectrum from *Great, take it. I just want to go and sit on a beach now* all the way to *You're stealing my baby, how dare you.*

Kieran's worked in two firms since graduating from university all those years ago, and audited many more. On reflection, he sees broadly three types of employees everywhere. There's the ones who count down the minutes and seconds to 5 pm and then flee. Every single day. Presenteeism. The worst. Why do it to yourself? Then there's the creeps and smarmers. The vipers. The kiss up and kick downers. The ones you really wouldn't want to get trapped in a lift with. And then there's the drones who stay till 8 pm. The ones who take their work home, the ones who against all the odds are trying to make some kind of difference. He's sure this company will be just as nice and just as horrible as all the other teams he's met. Maybe it's himself who needs the beach, he thinks...

Back in his own office in New Town, Kieran drops onto his desk all the files the managing director – a very pleasant chap in the end – gave him, and sinks into his chair. There's something very comforting about your own chair in an organisation, he thinks. Home from home. His boss and CEO, Mark, puts his head around the office door. "How did it go? Worth pursuing?", he asks. Mark is late 50s, florid, and self-made as he tells everyone. He's also captain of his local golf club and used to getting his way. He keeps on talking of retiring and handing over the reins but Kieran has long stopped believing him.
Kieran shrugs. "That's what we'll find out," he gestures at the pile of documents.
"Good, good. Got a minute?"
Kieran nods, "Of course, come on in."
"Actually, I thought we'd go out somewhere. Grab a coffee." Mark seems more nervous than Kieran's used to seeing him.

A short while later, they settle into a quiet coffee shop on Dundas Street. Kieran looks at his boss, "What's up?"

Mark shuffles his mug to one side and leans on the table between them. "This is how it is. And it's not easy to say this. Not easy at all. Specially as we're friends and all..."

"You're firing me?", asks Kieran with a smile.

"No, no, not at all," replies Mark with a look of horror. "Well, I don't know. Sort of. Maybe."

"Mark, this isn't like you. Spit it out. I won't be upset," offers Kieran gently.

Mark looks up at the ceiling, around them, and then straight at Kieran. He leans in further, and continues, barely whispering, "The planned merger with Vortex Dynamics... It looks like it might turn out to be more of a buyout than we thought. I'm staying on in some kind of purely ceremonial role for a year or so... But it'll leave us with two CFOs..."

"One more than is needed."

"Yes, exactly. On the nail as ever. Now, we're happy to go through a straight interview process to select the best candidate – you, obviously – but I suspect the odds may be stacked against you. I don't have the deciding vote."

"And you'd prefer not to go through such a...visible process."

Mark leans back into his chair and nods. He looks around him as Kieran reflects. "I knew we should have gone for a beer," he jokes half-heartedly.

"There would be a payout?", asks Kieran, his head tilted to one side.

"Enormous," promises Mark.

"There would be a handover period?"

"Completely your call, your terms," Mark opens his hands wide.

"I get to take my chair?"

"Whatever office furniture you want."

Kieran looks at his friend. "Thank you. This must be hard for you."

Mark shifts in his seat uncomfortably and smiles feebly.

"You know what? Done. But I go today. In fact, I go now." Kieran grins and stands up.

"Now? But...but what are you going to do?," asks Mark in some surprise.

"I'm going to be true to myself like I've been told. I'm going to write a book."

And with a glint in his eye and a *toodle-oo* worthy of Bertie Wooster, Kieran strolls out of the coffee shop.

This is what it feels like, he thinks to himself.

"Thanks, Mauricio, but seriously, best thing that ever happened to me. Without a question," says Kieran to his eldest son down the phone. "No....no, I'm not going to sue for unlawful dismissal. Why should I? I've had a good career. I'm 56. *Carpe diem* and all that. I never wanted to be CEO. I told Mark that many.... Yes, sure. I'll see you at the weekend if you're in town. We'll get a round of golf in. Sure. Be well," Kieran largely shouts the last bit down the line as he suspects Mauricio's already hung up. Not for the first time, Kieran marvels at the differences between his three children.

Kieran turns back to the empty screen. Out the window he watches a plane fly west high up in the distance, its contrails long and thin in the sky. *Not much wind today*, he thinks to himself. A seagull swoops by with a long twig in its beak. *I wonder where it's building a nest*, he thinks to himself. Somewhere out of sight he hears a car horn and then an answering shout. *Traffic's getting worse around here*, he thinks to himself...

Kieran looks at the empty screen and then turns to check on Harmony in her cot behind him. Gabriella's out at singing classes or something, he remembers. He does a double take on seeing his granddaughter standing leaning on the cot railing, watching him intently. He could swear he sees Silvia in her gaze.

Chastened, Kieran swivels back to face his laptop. After a long beat, he writes, *I am authentic. I'm doing what I'm meant to be doing*. He spins round to Harmony triumphantly, but she's lying back down, fast asleep.

Kieran frowns, thinking to himself, *Tough crowd*. But as he turns once more to his screen, he's grinning.

Self-Reflection
1. What has been Kieran's learning so far?

2. Is there anything you do where you are fully in flow, where time seems to pass without you realising it?
3. What do you currently do that's not true to who you really are (or want to be)?
4. What could you do about this?

5. Jacqui Loosens Up

For the nth time this shift, Jacqui feels like screaming at someone. On this occasion it's the teenage daughter of a cancer patient. Her father has, Jacqui reckons, maybe a day or two left and yet the girl sits by his bedside texting the world, oblivious it seems. In a better mood, she'd probably reflect it's the daughter's way of dealing with the situation, but Jacqui hasn't slept more than a few hours in the last couple of days.

Jacqui's a palliative care nurse in an oncology ward. She sees a lot of suffering and a lot of death. She also sees unimaginable positivity and acts of true bravery on most shifts. It's what keeps her going when the Furies circle. Today is one of the exceptions.

This is not how it was supposed to play out. They were supposed to grow old together, she and Silvia. 80s disco nights, Cuba Libres in the Caribbean, giggles in bed under the covers, and then maybe one day, if they really had to, rocking chairs side by side. Their life together defined to Jacqui who she is. Was. Silvia hasn't kept her side of the deal.

Meaning well, friends had said her experience and skills must have helped, but if anything they'd made it worse. She'd known day by day how Silvia was dropping further away from life. At any point she could map out the remainder of the journey, all the way to the end. Of course, Silvia had been fearless. Well, most of the time. Jacqui can feel the clouds gathering again and she breathes out hard. Tries to let the darkness go.

Silvia, Silvia, Silvia. Jacqui thinks of her cowbell and the card at home. *I am loose* and also *Break free and jump*. That's all the card said. Batshit *loca* doesn't come close, thinks Jacqui and finally she smiles, the first time in a long while.

"Think it's funny my Dad's dying, do you?", snarls the teenage girl watching her.

Jacqui frowns.

Jacqui wanders along the empty beach. It's a cold, windy morning in late March and even the dogwalkers are giving the sands a miss today. Gullane was one of their favourites. A long, open beach with little coves on either side. In truth, the beach doesn't end. It just keeps going around headlands and outcrops to Aberlady one way and North Berwick the other.

If my parents could just see me now, thinks Jacqui to herself. As a child, she'd hated the cold. She'd never been able to understand why her parents, her mother round with Jacqui, had emigrated from Trinidad to Scotland of all places. This was about as far from the islands as you could get. Maybe that was it. A lot later in life she'd discovered that her beloved Dad was not her biological father. Something had happened back in Port-of-Spain, but her mother refused to discuss it, and her father kept silent out of respect for her.

They too had gone, five years ago and within months of each other. Suddenly feeling very old and very alone, Jacqui says to herself, *Lucky people*, and immediately regrets it. Silvia hated self-pity.

And really, she considers, what does she have to feel sorry about? Yes, she's just lost her partner, but otherwise it hasn't been too hard a life. She hasn't been affected by war. Hasn't walked through deserts and drifted across seas to be here. Hasn't lost limbs. Hasn't lost herself and her world to drugs. Hasn't… Against all this, Jacqui might hold up that being Black and gay in Edinburgh hasn't always been a barrel of laughs, even within her own devoutly Christian family. Jacqui stops by the water's edge. Somewhere out across the sea is Fife, but the weather's too grey for her to see its low cliffs and shoreline. *Dreich* indeed. A good Scots word. If there's one thing Jacqui does know it's herself. She knows who she is, what she likes, what's important to her, what's meaningful to her, what she's good at…

And what she's not good at is change. She joined the NHS straight out of school, studied part-time to get her degree, and worked her way up to a level of seniority she felt comfortable with and no higher. She's stayed in oncology all the way through, has never thought of going private or doing anything else. She understands how the rhythm and routine sustain her. Knowing where everything is, what to do when this or that happens, who to page, who will need a hug, who will need to be left alone… When you've been doing this for thirty years, there are few surprises.

Jacqui accepts she's a dinosaur in many ways. The world is different to when she started out. There's constantly new language we're creating and learning where the polarisation alarms her. The vitriol seeps into gender and status and pronouns and independence and who is most worthy and... We multiscreen to hide and shout. We...

Jacqui grins. Silvia had always been amazed by how stuck in the wool she was. She'd be in hysterics if she could hear Jacqui's train of thought now.

Jacqui's not good at change and yet Silvia's passing has forced change on her.

Jacqui's not good at change and yet change is what she desperately needs.

Jacqui looks across at her counsellor. Things have got so grim recently that she was even sent home from one shift. Jacqui likes to think she and everyone in the NHS are all in the same boat. Everyone's been running on empty through Covid for so long now. But somewhere she knows it's more than that.

Jacqui's counsellor is probably the same age as her. Short spiky brown hair above little round glasses above a very drab blouse above grey trousers above equally sensible shoes. *Girl needs a bit more colour in her life*, Jacqui can't help thinking.

Counselling was something she and Silvia had discussed. Jacqui was the professional, the one who had seen it all, yet it was Silvia who looked after her towards the end. She made sure everything was in place, all the admin and legal stuff sorted. They had six years together. *Not enough, not nearly enough*, thinks Jacqui yet again.

The counsellor leans in, "What would you like to cover today?"

Jacqui looks at the woman and wonders what she has seen in this so carefully arranged room. If it compares in any way to what she sees in her ward every shift. She feels guilty for this thought, reminds herself that there's no competition when it comes to suffering. It's how you react to something, not the event itself, that's important. This is the mantra she repeats to herself.

"Something needs to change," begins Jacqui. "I need to change. And I'm scared, really scared. How about we start there?"

The counsellor pushes her glasses back and smiles at her encouragingly.

Maybe this wasn't such a truly bad idea after all.

A month or so later and life has moved on. As a first step, Jacqui has cut her hours down at work to half. She's signed up for interim nursing bank work in case she ever needs some extra cash, but so far she hasn't taken up any of the shifts she's been offered. Her colleagues were initially a little surprised – Jacqui's always been the person to go to if you needed someone to cover your shift – but they can't deny the change in her. "I think they're more than a wee bit envious," was how Jacqui had described it to her counsellor with a smile at her most recent session.

Today marks another step. Silvia had drawn an enormous amount of pleasure and meaning from working with refugees in her spare time. Maybe it came from her own family's experience of fleeing Chile and the support they received. Through several discussions with her counsellor, Jacqui had come to see it as a way of keeping Silvia's work going and also giving herself a way forward. Sometimes we can take the vision of our heroes and make them authentically our own. "And it certainly beats hiding from the world," she'd offered to her counsellor, who Jacqui was pleased to see did have a sense of humour after all.

Jacqui stands in front of the community hall a few streets away from her flat. Today is an outreach event for refugees to meet locals in the area and vice versa. Baby steps for all concerned. Coffee and cakes will be provided, she'd been assured.

Jacqui has volunteered to work with the group from a health care perspective. Giving advice about who to contact, what to do, how to register for services, all that kind of stuff. She wonders who and what she will find inside. What stories, what experiences, what traumas, what needs. She can't imagine what lives she'll learn.

Silvia would no doubt have flown right in, introduced herself to everyone, and had everyone joking and laughing within minutes. Yet still Jacqui hangs back by the entrance. She contemplates going for another walk around the block first.

"We going in?", asks her counsellor with a gentle smile as she stubs her cigarette out by a bin. Jacqui has completely forgotten they'd agreed to go together this first time.

Jacqui nods and with a quick look up at the heavens for support, she walks into the hall.

Self-Reflection
1. Why do you think change is such an issue for Jacqui?
2. How are you with change?
3. What helps you through change?
4. What do you think of Jacqui's mantra that the reaction to an event is more important than the event itself?

6. Ignacio Holds His Hands Up

As a child, Ignacio can't remember when or where exactly, he'd come across the Hebrew phrase *tikkun olam*. Heal the world. It's still pretty strange to him that he can't recall how he found out about it, because he'd immediately thought it so cool that it's been his lodestar, his mission ever since.

Charismatic when he wants to be, charm has not typically been an overriding concern for Ignacio. If he's never going to win any awards for his bedside manner, he's undeniably a skilled hand surgeon. He see patients as primarily cases to be resolved, and so he focuses exclusively on what he can control, not on the more complex human above the wrist. Such single-minded dedication to his trade has seen two wives come and quickly go along the way. This isn't something he's proud of, but he doesn't pretend it keeps him up at nights either. Several patents and a decade of successful private practice mean that he doesn't need to keep working for the money. Similarly, a couple of well received papers have ensured that his reputation is impregnable. And so, despite everything, if he were to take a long, true look at himself in the mirror, Ignacio would probably admit he's bored. Maybe this is why he was so thrown this morning by a patient in her sixties. Mrs McRae was her name. After listening in an unmistakably dubious silence to his step by step outline of her upcoming procedure, she'd suddenly reached out and taken his own hand in hers. She'd turned it over to study his palm.

"Hmmm," she'd said. "I thought so." And that was it. No explanation, no sop for his curiosity.

Ignacio stands on his balcony and looks out over night-time Edinburgh. He takes a sip from his Glenmorangie and holds his palm up to the light spilling out from the room behind him. It seems like a pretty normal hand to him. *And I reckon I've seen more than a few in my time*, he reminds himself. Nevertheless, for some reason the chain of thoughts takes him to his sister and her mysterious card for him. *I have a mission.* And then there was the task she'd set him. *Find the child who wanted to heal the world.*

Ignacio leans on the railings and wonders yet again what his dear old sister means by this.

From inside he hears the doorbell ring. Dinner has arrived. With one last look at his palm, he knocks back the whisky and heads indoors to find his wallet.

When Ignacio needs to think, he gets on his bike and heads off over the bridge to North Queensferry and then east along the coast for as long as the mood takes him. It may be March but the sun's visible at least and the wind's not as bitterly fierce as it can be at this time of the year.

Ignacio finds cycling very clearing. Some get this from mountains, others from the sea, but he's always enjoyed open roads. Bikes, motor bikes, cars, anything mechanical. A terrible sense of direction means his rides often become full-blown expeditions, but funnily enough, this is the one area of his life in which he does love to be surprised. It's good sometimes to suspend control and get lost. Today his mind's full after a long week of consultations and he's out beyond Aberdour before the weight starts to fall away. He does have a mission, he keeps thinking to himself. He always has. *Tikkun olam*. *Tikkun olam*. He can't even begin to estimate how many hands he's saved over the years. How many people still have grip and touch because of him. His research and designs have helped countless more across the world. So why does he now feel like that's not enough? That there's something missing?

Ignacio swerves past a couple pushing their pram in the middle of the cycle path, both deeply absorbed in their phones. He's always thought that if he'd ever had kids he'd have been the most attentive father ever.

And that was the other thing. *Go and find the child...* Well, if she wanted a child found, he could certainly do that. On the spur of the moment, Ignacio takes his hands off the handlebars and starts to swoop from side to side, giggling at the sheer fun of it all after the miles of unrelenting pedalling so far. He holds his hands up high above him and whoops into the wind. From side to side he goes until, almost inevitably, he comes round a corner just as a woman in a big orange coat steps up from a bench by the side of the path. Ignacio instinctively leans the bike away from her, but as he does so, his front wheel hits a ridge in the tarmac and slides away from him. Down goes Ignacio in a sliding, rolling ball as the bike clatters to the ground.

Dazed, he lies on the path for a moment getting his breath back. The woman rushes over, "*O dios mío*, I'm so sorry," she starts off apologetically but then switches tone, "you know though, that was really stupid. Some would say you deserved... Ah, you're bleeding. Don't move." The voice softens while also becoming more professional. "It's OK, I'm a doctor." And she crouches down to examine Ignacio's left knee.

"You don't need to. I'm also a...," begins Ignacio.

"Shush! Stay still," the woman reprimands him.

Ignacio's not used to being shushed but is surprised to find he's not too angry about it. He looks at the woman studying and now lightly brushing bits of gravel away from the wound on his knee. She's no more than a few years younger than him, black hair streaked with grey, and with a pointy nose that he can't call anything other than irresistible. "That's a nice coat. Better not get any blood or bike oil on it," he observes sensibly if somewhat randomly.

The woman ignores him before finally straightening back up. "You'll survive." She eyes him coolly. "But I think your bike's gone to a better world." She points her chin at the buckled front wheel.

"Sod it," Ignacio can't help himself. "That wheel cost... Well, it doesn't matter." He gingerly gets to his feet and quickly runs his hands over his torso to see if there's any other damage. Satisfied, he bends down to pull his bike over to prop it up against the bench. The movement makes him feel giddy and so he sits down on the wooden seat, a little more heavily than he meant to.

The woman leans down next to him and reaches over, "Let's take your helmet off. Looks like you may have hit your head on the way down."
And with that, Ignacio passes out.

Ignacio looks at his bike sitting on its front forks in his entrance hall. It needs some TLC but otherwise it's fine, all things considered. A bit like him apparently, though he still feels pretty groggy.
It had been strange being a patient in his own hospital. Once it had got out about how he'd ended up there the team had been merciless. He knows it's going to take a long time to live this one down. But in truth, looking back at it now, he's quite touched by the ribbing he got. He hadn't been aware of the warmth he enjoys despite his repeated failure to remember anyone's birthday or even if they have children or spouses or any kind of life at all outside the operating room.
When he passed out, Lucía had called an ambulance, though he was already conscious again by the time it turned up. She'd followed behind with his bike, waited all the way through the check up, and had then even brought him home. She'd mumbled something about feeling guilty for contributing to the accident, and handed him her card – in the unlikely event he ever forgot her name, she'd joked badly – before leaving rather hesitantly about an hour ago.
Ignacio contemplates the card now. He hadn't realised people still gave out business cards, but clearly he was mistaken. *Dra. Lucía*

Jiménez, Directora, Orfanato de Los Ángeles, La Habana, Cuba. He puts the card in his pocket, considers against his own medical advice a stiff drink to calm his nerves, and reluctantly settles instead for a hefty glass of tap water.

Suitably refreshed, Ignacio sinks into his extraordinarily expensive sofa and looks back over his day. His sister's death has, if anything, only strengthened his view that our time on this small blue planet is invariably limited. For Ignacio, each day should contain some element of achievement, some element of growth however small from the previous one.

The quest to define such an achievement has become more and more difficult recently. He may only be 51 but in reality he's already achieved everything he'd thought would make him successful and fulfilled. Happy, that's a different question. He's never expected happiness. Silvia might have had it, he acknowledges. Strangely, given all she went through. But for himself, not a driving pursuit.

Professional expertise? Tick. Peer respect? Tick. Financial freedom and most if not all the luxuries you can buy? Tick. A lifetime of treating other people's medical issues to the best of his *tikkun olam* ability? Another resounding tick.

So maybe we can give him a break when we look at him now, sitting on his sofa and wondering just what on earth he should do for the rest of his life.

Ignacio fingers the card in his pocket.

"Mrs McRae? It's Dr Ignacio here. I wanted to tell you myself. I had a small accident on my bike yesterday and I'm afraid we're going to have to…", Ignacio leans back in the chair in his home office, absent-mindedly playing with the cord for the window blinds.

His patient interrupts him. "Postpone the operation? Yes, I was expecting it."

"You were?"

"Umhm. It was all there. In your hand. I'll see you next week then?"

"Yes…that's the plan," Ignacio stumbles, a little disconcerted.

"Good. Be nice to her." Ignacio can feel her smile down the line.

"Who?"

"You know," and she hangs up.

Ignacio stares at his phone in wonder. He puts it down and pulls the blinds wide open. He raises his palms up to the sunlight to inspect them.

Self-Reflection

1. What options do you see for Ignacio going forward?
2. Where are the gaps if any in his life?
3. How do you think you'd feel if you achieved everything you'd set out to do?
4. How does *tikkun olam* resonate with you?

7. Mauricio Has A Setback

Someone's knocking on a door somewhere. Mauricio wonders, in sequence of growing consciousness:

1. *Am I late for something?*
2. *What time is it?*
3. *And where am I?*

He's proud of the fact that even when stirring from sleep, he has marshalled and packaged the required information into no more than three elements like all good consultants should. He's less impressed that his first thought was more of a panic reaction than might be hoped.

Mauricio sits up in the (his?) bed and establishes, in reverse sequence now, that he's in a hotel room, it's 5.16pm, and so by deduction he is not late for anything.

5.16. That means he's only been asleep for just over an hour, even if it feels like someone's knocked him on the side of the head with a caber. The combination of jet lag and lack of sleep generally is calling the shots today.

Mauricio gets to his feet, finds a towel, and goes to answer his room door. By the time he gets there, whoever it was has disappeared leaving a bag of neatly ironed and folded shirts on his doorstep. Mauricio whistles softly at the speed of service, calculating the time it must have taken for all the various steps to happen in his shirt dry cleaning process. *Stellar*, he thinks, and mentally files a promise to give the hotel a five-star review later. He almost certainly won't get round to doing so, but it's the thought that counts, as he likes to remind himself.

Back in the room, Mauricio eyes up the minibar. He's not meeting his client in the reception area downstairs till seven, so surely a pick me up would go some way to easing the caber blow? It would indeed. Now, where was the presentation printout?

Hanoi's a suitably frenetic city for his current state, Mauricio considers. He feels like he's in the middle of the large roundabout outside his hotel with the hundreds of scooters constantly flying round it and veering off in all different directions. Watching the night-time traffic play out below him from the terrace bar, Mauricio tries to discern where the chaos stops and the organisation starts. It seems a very fine line.

He turns back to his client, who's calmly watching him over an espresso. Eyeing his own empty whisky glass, Mauricio gestures, "Another?", at the coffee.

The client, a Vietnamese man the age of Mauricio's father, shakes his head. He'd volunteered his first name – Hanh or Khanh, Mauricio can't remember which – at the start of the evening. "Your company," starts the man, "has been very helpful to us over the years. We owe a lot of our success to the advice we've received." There doesn't seem to be a flicker of emotion in his face.

Mauricio nods his appreciation, wondering:

1. *Where's the waiter gone?*
2. *Where's he going with this?*
3. *How soon can I make my getaway without being rude?*

The man sighs ever so faintly, as if aware of Mauricio's thoughts. "They must trust you a lot for such a big contract so far from home." The client's look goes distant as he leans back and away from the terrace light.

"Well," says Mauricio in a tone he hopes is reassuring. "I've been client facing for a fair few years now. True, this is my first engagement in Sai..Hanoi, but I spend 90% of my time on the road. Lots of air miles," he smiles.

"Many places. It must be hard to focus," states the man blandly. Mauricio can't help shuffling his chair forward to better see his face. The air hangs muggy and sticky.

"Cleantech is a big field to play in these days," offers Mauricio, still trying to read the situation. "Asia's finally waking up to it." He immediately regrets the remark as the man frowns.

"True, nowadays there are more players in the market as you say." The client taps out a cigarette from his box. He lights it without making any show of offering one to Mauricio.

The thought comes to Mauricio that he's booked his flight out too early the following afternoon. He'll have to cut short his day in the client's premises somehow. There's been no mention so far of tomorrow's schedule so maybe he could pretend... And then it suddenly dawns on him. "Are you dropping us?", he asks directly.

For the first time this evening, the client's face lights up with a brief smile. "Astute. So that's why they trust you. I was hoping to discuss this with someone more… But yes, I regret to say we have decided to move forward henceforth with a more local advisory service." The client pauses to take a long drag on his cigarette and to study Mauricio. "There are more players indeed." He pushes his chair back and gets to his feet without waiting for a response. "I trust you'll enjoy our little city before you go. There is much for the foreigner to see and do."

Mauricio's ex-client bows his head slightly and walks off towards the stairs.

It's several hours later and Mauricio's very drunk. He feels like he's drowning in a vat of churning butter, unable to get enough purchase on the steep and slippery sides to pull himself out. It's not the greatest of feelings.

Some wise impulse has led him to leave the hotel bar and head out into the night. *There is much for the foreigner to see and do.* He's now very lost in a city he knows only from dated war films. Long muted, his phone keeps vibrating with increasingly irate messages from his boss back in London. He stopped reading these texts shortly after leaving the hotel. He's yet to reply to any of them.

A Japanese style *izakaya* looms up in front of him and he gratefully ploughs through the curtains to a stool by the bar. "Mekong whisky *o negai shimasu,*" he slurs to the barman. He smiles with pleasant surprise at his recollection of the few words he picked up that time he went to see his brother David in Hokkaido.

Like everyone else in Mauricio's life it seems, the barman coolly studies him for a long beat before finally pouring and pushing forward a small shot of whisky. The manner is one of extreme reluctance.

"*Shukran,*" mutters Mauricio incongruously and downs it in one. He sits at the bar staring into space, trying hard to refocus enough so that he can pull back together the various strands of his day so far. He places his palms flat on the counter in search of some kind of grounding.

David. David and his world of arcane cultural rites. His bubblegum brain sister Gabriella. Someone has to be professional in this generation, he sniffs. Someone has to be sensible. And now Dad wanting to be a writer... Uncle Ignacio's the only one who's got his head at all screwed on. Not that he ever sees him.

The consulting gig's been fun, even as he feels the hunger and the ambition drain away through sheer exhaustion. And at barely 32, there are already younger hotshots rapidly rising through the ranks behind him. He has dreams of starting his own boutique consultancy focussed on a couple of key clients, but doesn't feel he could do it alone. The trouble is he has few friends in the trade. Connections are too fleeting, and most of his uni mates are now too busy cohabiting and populating.

It's a strange world. Mauricio spends his whole time looking to help other people with their problems. And yet he'd never dream of asking anyone for help with his own. He helps build other people's futures while being light with his own.

And somewhere he understands that he needs helps sorting this out first. He wouldn't call it recklessness, but there's an insouciance, a come what may which plays out in a taste for risk he can't hide from. And the only person he would even have considered asking for help is no longer around to do so. She knew this, so he doesn't understand why she's now instructing him to *Surround yourself with love*. It all seems a bit pointless.

Mauricio realises it's been a while since his phone last vibrated. Perhaps he's finally safe. He puts a hand into his jacket but the pocket's empty. As are all his other pockets. His wallet too has disappeared.

He looks at the barman, who returns his gaze evenly.

Mauricio grins and runs.

Self-Reflection
1. What advice would you give Mauricio?
2. What would increase the chances of him paying heed to this advice?
3. How comfortable are you with reaching out for support?
4. Who would you reach out to?

8. Henry Looks At A Map

Henry studies the view indicator for a moment to see where Edinburgh lies. The arrow on the metal plaque nailed to the stone plinth shows his home to be directly behind him. Henry turns but that whole side of the mountain is now shrouded in mist. Although it's July and relatively warm for these parts, the clouds have swooped back in and the views are pulling shorter and shorter.

The Cairngorms in Scotland's highlands are known as much for their majesty as for their capricious weather. The exposed plateau around Ben Macdui, the second highest mountain in the UK, has a highest recorded wind gust of 176 mph. Conditions can deteriorate rapidly and unexpectedly. Even in the middle of summer, small patches of snow can be found in gullies and corridors. Earlier today, Henry had been startled by the sudden whoop-whoop of blades as a yellow rescue helicopter had shot over and away. A faller by the Northern Corries, said a passing walker.

Still, it's been a relatively simple day so far. A long approach and traverse up the flank of Cairn Lochan, across streams and some boggy patches lower down before rising onto the plateau and its stony paths. A small group of deer had raised their heads at him as he approached over one incline. They'd eyed him up and moved slowly off, not too bothered but equally not too keen to be close either. He used to think it was unusual to find deer so high, but apparently during the summer months they climb to avoid the midges and flies.

The summit is broad and surprisingly rounded for such a relatively high peak. Hikers continue to appear from several different routes up. Set by Aviemore and its large ski centre, it's not a mountain to climb if you're looking for peace and solitude. Cairns and windbreaks of different sizes crowd around the main trig point.

Keen for his lunch, Henry finds a pile of stones off on his own to one side. In front of him, Cairn Toul rises across the glacier-carved trench of the Lairig Ghru. Everywhere he looks, as the clouds part and collect again, the world of his childhood with his father looms up.

Like him, his father had been a solicitor. Indeed, Henry is now the third generation of solicitors to work for the firm that carries his family name. He will be the last. His daughter Josie has chosen her own path as an architect, something he's immensely proud of, even if he can't deny that for him law has been a good career. A Writer to the Signet as solicitors used to be known in Edinburgh. An honourable pursuit, and he has no regrets at all on that front.

With his father, though, Henry's always felt he's lived a little in the shadow. A larger than life character, Henry's dad had seemed to practise law purely as a sideshow to his bigger interest of mountaineering. Though he'd dragged Henry in his childhood up any number of Munros - mountains in Scotland over 3000 feet - these were really only warm-up acts for higher adventures further afield in the Alps, the Pyrenees, and later the Himalayas.

The humdrum minutiae of law were not for such a character, who preferred a big cause and a juicy case to anything too pedestrian or intricate. It had been he who had gone to war for Guillermina and her children's right to reside in Scotland. Even now, Henry can't help thinking the nobility of that endeavour probably had more than its fair share of vanity stirred in. He's also always wondered if Dad had had a bit of a thing for Guillermina too.

Munching on his tuna wrap, Henry studies his map once more. Satisfied, he then digs into his rucksack for a scarf. His father had eventually paid the price for his passion. A rockfall below the south face of Annapurna, frequent but unpredictable, had taken him and his climbing partner just above Base Camp when Henry was in his teens. There was a time when Henry, quiet and methodical, had felt he must be something of a disappointment to those who knew his father. That burning energy and constant activity had skipped him by to land instead in his daughter, who now runs him ragged with her fretting and juggling of a myriad balls.

A couple in their twenties come over to him, disturbing his thoughts. "Could you take a picture of us?"

Henry nods and smiles. This turns into a frown as he sees they only have a small bottle of Coke between them. In trainers and shorts, they're dressed more for a stroll down Aviemore High Street than for the mountains. He scans the surrounding conditions yet again. They should be OK but still... Henry takes the requested photo, adding as he passes the phone back, "You may want to have something a trifle warmer as back up next time. Some more water too. It can change quickly up here."

The young man winks his thanks for the photo and mutters, "Sure," noncommittally and without meeting Henry's eye. The two slope off to catch the view from another side, giggling as they go.

A woman in her fifties and with a black and white collie at her side nods at him from a little way away. "Numpties, eh? Eejits like that keep us from our warm beds looking for their cold bodies. You were more polite than I'd have bothered being." She harrumphs and bends down to cuddle her dog.

Henry shoulders his bag, tilts his head to the woman in goodbye, and starts off for the second and last Munro of the day, Cairn Gorm. The peak is directly above the ski centre. Runs and lifts climb its flanks, so it probably won't be the most scenic of summits, but at least the way up is along the Northern Corries and their craggy edges. If the clouds clear, the views should be astounding.

The track takes him back along his outward route up to Ben Macdui before heading off to the right and around a small lochan. The path is empty and undemanding, and he soon settles into a long, regular stride.

The memory of his father and of Guillermina takes him to Silvia and her own family. Although his father had been active on their case, Henry had not met Silvia till she came to him last year, keen to get a will in place as well as her odd requests. She'd graciously said that as he was part of her story in a way, it seemed only right to come to him.

He'd found her charming and brave. It had stirred a lot of feelings in him, feelings which even now threaten to bring a tear to his eye.

Henry too had lost his wife Isabel early. To leukaemia, three months to the day from her diagnosis. He'd been left with a young daughter to bring up on his own, something which he knows had saved him and got him through the pain. *And now this young girl has grown up and is making life hell for this old man,* smiles Henry to himself.

The terms of Silvia's will have proved relatively straightforward so far. As instructed, he'd forwarded David funds for his flight to Chile. There are also funds to be transferred if Gabriella gets into acting school, but he's not heard from her or from Kieran on this yet. The only minor intervention has been to quietly secure Mauricio's release from a police station cell in Hanoi. They young man had evidently had a drop too much to drink.

Henry feels a few spatters of water fall on his bare head and scans the clouds. Just a passing shower, unexpected but wet all the same. He reaches for a rain jacket. *Planning, planning, planning,* as his father would have said. Henry smiles, quietly proud of himself. Walkers in the mountains often talk of a mysterious feeling of being accompanied on their walks. Ben Macdui in particular has the legend of the Old Grey Man, a wandering figure hidden in the mists. And so it is with Henry. Up here in the mountains is where he feels his father's presence strongest.

Henry stops putting on his jacket in sudden awe as an osprey floats over a crest in front of him. The bird, with its magnificent white chest and long brown wings, eyes him before drifting off and away over the gorge.

Henry marvels at this sight all for himself on the mountainside.

Self-Reflection
1. What qualities do you see in Henry?
2. Which voices from your past do you sometimes hear in your head?
3. When you are setting out on a new challenge, how mindful are you of planning first?
4. In general, do you like to follow a set path or wander as the mood takes you?

Part Two

"Develop enough courage so that you can stand up for yourself and then stand up for somebody else."

Maya Angelou

9. David Digs Deeper

Like many ancient cultures, the Mapuche have a myth around an end of the world flood from which all will be cleansed and recreated. Order between water and earth is only restored when there's one couple left. Scanning the clouds, David darkly wonders whether the recent months of cold, hard rain have been a preparation for that. Still, it's October now and summer should be coming to Chiloé. Things have moved on from where we left our hero. The planned stay for a few months with his *abuela* in Chile has turned into a Master's at Universidad de Los Lagos in Castro, Chiloé's main city. David likes to think there's a purpose to this and not that he's merely postponing having to get a job. He is at least working for his living, more or less. English teaching takes care of the day to day expenses. A loan is covering the university costs.

He sees his grandmother most weekends. It's not a very long drive down the Panamerican Highway to her home in Quellón, and the Cadillac likes a cruise. Maybe the biggest news is that he and Montse are living together. When he got his place at the university, she'd announced that her research and teaching could be done from Castro. They'd looked at each other and that was that. Guillermina had celebrated the news with them, adding that her grandson's presence in the house had been cramping her style with her friends anyway.

David smiles at the thought. He's sitting under an awning in a café on the Plaza de Armas, Castro's main square. He's just said goodbye to one of his private students, a telecoms engineer looking to emigrate to the US. With a lingering look, she'd invited him to a party that night, but David had made his excuses. Today's the first month anniversary of him and Montse living together, and he's cooking her a Scots meal in celebration. He's still trying to work out what the closest ingredients he can find might be.

David hasn't had many serious relationships in his life. A girlfriend from school hadn't survived the transition to university, and then a girl he went out with for the duration of his second year at uni had left him for someone with a more promising future, as she'd coolly informed him.

Montse's a whole different ballgame. Two years older than him at 24, David can find it hard not to feel overawed by her clarity. To him, Montse always knows what she believes in, what's important to her, what she wants, where she's going...

David thinks back yet again to his mother and her task for him, *Take me home and find yourself.* On their road trip around Chile – and some of Bolivia and Argentina too – they'd decoded and broken down together what finding yourself might include. They'd agreed it was more than simply where you were born and your culture. It came down to values and influences and beliefs and childhood stories too. Montse could list out answers for herself in all these areas. She'd told him how having and embracing this knowledge gave her strength. *Mum would have absolutely adored her,* thinks David fondly.

In terms of the task, he thinks he's getting there. The first part at least. To his Scottish heritage he can now add the Chilean side in much fuller detail. As he's dug deeper, it's been fascinating to see how Chilean and Huilliche his mother was. Before, it had just been her way. Mum's thing. Now, as he's learnt more and more about her people and their ways, he can see how influenced his mother was by it all. And in turn, yes, it's a part of his story too. Not as much – it's likely he'll always be more *gringo* than Chilean – but it's there nevertheless.

The rest of it, he's still working on. Over a pisco sour in Punta Arenas, by the Strait of Magellan and the southernmost city in Chile, Montse had outlined her own plans. On the one hand she wants to finish her research, maybe take it forward in a university career. And on the other, she's strongly drawn to politics. "It's time for people our age to drive things forward," she'd declared. David doesn't doubt her passion and commitment on that front. "And you, David? Who are you?" That had been the telling question.

He looks at his watch and wonders where his firebrand is. Being late is part of who she is, but she's not usually this bad, thinks David, noting his own cultural prejudice.

He orders another coffee and goes over in his head once more a story he's looking to use with his students in class tomorrow. It's from the Haida, an indigenous group on the northwest coast of Canada and Alaska, and it relates how the raven stole the sun from the house of the old woodcutter. It's a beautiful story and David's looking forward to telling it to his class. Such legends have usually prompted the students to offer their own stories of *trauco* trolls, *sirena* mermaids and more, which David unashamedly notes down.

A shadow passes across him and Montse drops down into the chair opposite him. Surprised at the lack of a kiss or greeting, David eyes her. "That's not the face of someone eagerly looking forward to a true, soul-warming Scots dinner," he offers tentatively.

Montse raises her eyes to his and only manages to get out, "My father," before bursting into tears.

From her kitchen window, Guillermina watches the Cadillac drive up. She purses her lips and wonders how her grandson will be tonight. It's been nearly a month since Montse flew home to Tarragona to care for her father. A stroke and the resulting paralysis down his left side has left him needing fulltime attention. Separated from her mother since he came out years ago, it's fallen to Montse as the only child to provide this attention.

Guillermina goes and stands in her doorway to welcome David. "So, young man, how goes big city life?"

David smiles weakly. Castro has the population of a suburb in Edinburgh, itself not the most gargantuan of cities.

Guillermina studies the bags under his eyes as he walks in and hugs her. "Looks like you've picked up the Chilean disease of forgetting to sleep. How's that working for you?"

"Gives me more time to study," tries David to a particularly unimpressed harrumph from his grandmother.

"*Ya basta*. Enough. Sit down over there," orders Guillermina. With a sigh, she lowers herself slowly into her own chair opposite as he does so. She looks her grandson in the eye. "There's a Taoist proverb which goes, *When drinking water, think of the source.* I hear your mother in these words. Where are you with her task for you?"

David can't help looking beyond his grandmother to an alcove in which a small urn with Silvia's ashes has been placed.

"I think," starts David. "I think... Montse and I talked about this a lot. The roots, my roots, I believe, are clear to me. Where I come from, my heritage, my childhood influences, all that.... With who I am, my values, my beliefs... A work in progress," he frowns.

Guillermina leans back. She wishes she had a bat or a tennis racquet or anything to whack her grandson with. She seems to remember an English expression about blood from a stone or something like that. After a long pause, she observes, "When I look at you, I see someone who's endlessly curious about the world and everyone in it. I see your interest in different cultures. Not just your own but in all... I see someone who loves stories." Guillermina coughs and reaches for a glass of water before continuing. "I see someone who is a natural bridge between people. I also see someone who enjoys teaching, someone who values learning and all the growth it brings." She stops to let her words sink in. "Do you see what I and all who have walked on this land here before me see?"

David reflects and nods. "I think, on an unconscious level, this is why I chose the Master's. Maybe it'll become a PhD, I don't know. I don't know what the next step is."

Guillermina smiles. "Another Taoist proverb tells us take a step to see the next step."

David holds his hands up in surrender and laughs. "And the journey of a thousand steps starts with just one. I get the message. I didn't realise old *machis* knew their Tao too," he jokes.

His grandmother scowls at him in mock indignation. "My blood flows in you. You're as old as me, don't you forget it."

"And my blood flows in you, so you're as young as me," replies David, beaming.

"Who's the philosopher now?" Guillermina chortles at the thought and then she's all seriousness again. "If you'll excuse this old *machi*, my simple learning has been that if you know where your home is, you'll always have that foundation. For whatever you choose to do. And for most - yes, it's an easy, Disney cartoon truth - but for most, home is where the heart is. For me and your grandfather, that's always been here. For your mother, she was always between. Partly here, partly Scotland. For you...," she drifts off to study his reaction. "Montse's heart is in Spain. Where's yours?" The question comes as no more than a whisper.

David looks at his *abuela* for a long moment. He sees all her love and all her history. He sees the river going all the way back. Through him, his mother, his grandmother, and beyond. He basks in this warmth and then turns his eyes to the way ahead.

David jumps to his feet, takes her head in his hands, and kisses his grandmother on the forehead. He grins, *"Adelante siempre!,"* and runs out the door.

Ever forward.

David stands on a doorstep, trying to calm his nerves. When the door finally opens, he immediately announces, "Don't ask me how, but I've got haggis and neeps and... Och, you're not going to break into tears every time I cook dinner are you?"

And he grins even wider as he's pulled inside.

Self-Reflection
1. What values do you see in David?
2. Which of these do you share?
3. How do you live up to your values?
4. Which of your values are under-represented in your life currently?

10. Gabriella Takes A Step

"Willkommen, bienvenue, welcome. Fremde, étranger, stranger…"

Gabriella loves the lines. It's such a fantastic opening. So simple, yet when delivered well by the MC, the setting's immediately luscious, evocative, decadent.

"Glücklich zu sehen, je suis enchanté, happy to see you…"

It's October and they're already casting the big production for December. And there's only one role Gabriella wants to play in Cabaret. Lying in bed, she turns over in her mind how to make Sally Bowles hers and not just imitate Liza Minelli. Harmony stirs in her sleep over in her cot but doesn't wake. Bliss.

Gabriella's already lived up to the first part of her task. She's got onto the one-year programme at Acting Coach Scotland, and loving it. She's learning so much, exploring so many aspects of herself she never knew she had, pushing herself constantly to be better.

And yet, if getting into the school wasn't hard enough, every class seems to raise the bar even higher. She finds herself among such truly talented people that she can't help feeling at times that she doesn't belong, that something will happen and she'll be found out…

"Bleibe, reste, stay…"

Gabriella sighs and tries to banish the self-doubt far away. *I've got this*, she thinks to herself, and then thinks it once more to convince herself. The audition's a week away and most of the women in her year are going for Sally. Agents will be coming to the production so it's a big deal. Get yourself noticed and who knows what doors will open. Gabriella looks at the clock by her bed. 3.17am. *I've got this*, she thinks and turns over to try and sleep.

"*Willkommen, bienvenue, welcome. Im Cabaret, au Cabaret, to Cabaret.*"

It's the final day of rehearsals. Gabriella got the part of Sally Bowles. Of course she got the part. She was brilliant in the audition, absolutely nailed it with no sign of the nerves that were tearing through her underneath.

No, that's not true. The nerves are there before and after. During, it's like being submerged in a river, like being a musician lost in the flow of the music. She's never been able to pinpoint it exactly for others. How everything slows down, how everything else falls away. She's totally, totally in the moment. It's amazing, uncanny even, how fully she occupies the space, how she is whoever she's playing with every sinew and bone in her body. No, the nerves and everything else, they come in all other moments when she's not performing. When life is not so simple.

The afternoon rehearsal's going well. There's a real energy to everyone's performance even though there's no audience. It's as if everyone's shifted up a gear in view of the stakes on offer the next day.

At the end of a busy club scene involving most of the cast, the director calls for a break so that the stagehands can rearrange some of the furniture. As the actors mill round the edge of the stage to give the guys room to manoeuvre the tables and chairs, Gabriella does an impromptu twirl, still lost in Sally. All of a sudden she finds herself in thin air. Time seems to stop, as they always say it does in such moments. There is the stage off to one side above her and the orchestra pit somewhere down below her in the darkness. In between, for the briefest of moments, is Gabriella. Even in this shortest of seconds, the thought flashes across her synapses that she's sure she felt a hand in the small of her back when she was still on the edge of the stage.

"I've got this. I'm doing it." Leaning on her crutches, Gabriella's facing off with Theo, her director.
"With a badly twisted right ankle and on more painkillers than I thought the NHS stocked?", asks the man gently, one hand to his hipster beard.
"With a brace, with a bar stool, with a crutch. Whatever it takes. I've got this." Gabriella is firm. No one's taking Sally away from her.
Theo leans back and considers his options. Eventually, he smiles and nods. "We're on in just over two hours. Let's run through the script together to see what adjustments we'll need to make. Think the painkillers will last that long?"

Gabriella pulls out a big bottle of pills from her bag and grins back, a little wildly it has to be said.

Gabriella's backstage in the dressing room she shares with the other female actors. Everyone's finally left and she's on her own now. Her friends Becca and Teri have been and cried and gone. Her father's disappeared off to bring the car up to the stage door, while Ignacio and Mauricio have just wandered out to find him with all the bouquets she got.

To say Gabriella was great tonight is to do an injustice to the word great. Start somewhere north of awesome and just keep going higher. That's how great she was.

But the adrenaline and the elation are starting to wear off and all she can feel now is her ankle throbbing. Actually, she wishes it was just throbbing she could feel and not excruciating, searing, singeing pain. There's a knock on the door and an instant later, her director sticks his head into the room. "Got a moment? There's someone who'd like to meet you." Theo flashes his eyes wide in warning and beams at her, before pushing the door further open. "This is Antoine, an agent who kindly dropped into our little show tonight."

"Oh Theo, you make it sound so casual," Antoine, short and immaculately dressed, smiles at him thinly. "As if you hadn't begged and implored me to come and see this wonderful creature." And with this he turns his attention fully to Gabriella. "You and I," he says as he sinks himself into one of the empty chairs next to her, "have a lot to talk about."

Antoine turns to the director, who takes the hint and withdraws back out the door. Antoine swivels round again to Gabriella. "Now, where shall we begin?"

"OK, this time, just this once, I'll give you the excuse of the ankle," Sophie breathes through a cloud of smoke. She'd given up on the café they were due to meet in an hour earlier and is now sitting on a bench in Inverleith Park overlooking the duck pond and Edinburgh beyond.

Gabriella ignores the comment and drops / falls onto the bench beside her mentor.

"You're going to get all butch and muscly with those crutches," approves Sophie. "Lots of roles going in the action world these days." Gabriella rolls her eyes as she leans the crutches against the side of the bench next to her. She turns to Sophie and cocks an eyebrow. "Yes, yes, OK, don't be so needy. You were good on Friday. Don't think I've ever seen such a static Sally but you got her spirit and zest anyhow. Well done you," offers Sophie warmly though perhaps more flatly than her family and friends would have. Still, it's praise none the less. Gabriella nods her thanks. Sophie continues, "More importantly, how do you feel you did?"

Gabriella looks at the older woman and realises no one else has asked that question.

"I… I zoned out to be honest. The excitement, the stress, the painkillers… It's all a bit of a blur," she replies hesitantly. "OK, I think."

"So what could have been better?", Sophie asks patiently.

Gabriella thinks for a long time. "My singing?", she tries.

Sophie shrugs. "Maybe. You're never going to be the strongest singer, but I thought you were fine. Enough for the part anyway." She looks hard at her mentee. "Gabi, you've got the focus and the passion and the love for what you do. Which is great. You're at least halfway there. Without those we wouldn't even be talking… Yet… What we always need to remember is that acting's a skill, a butch old muscle even. Something we can always make stronger. You go to a different place when you're on it, Gabi, which I love, but what you also need to do is keep just a smidgen of yourself in the picture too. Almost like you're watching yourself perform. It's an awareness of what you're doing and all that's going on around you." Sophie pauses for a moment to take a long drag on her cigarette. "There were a couple of cues you missed from the guy playing Brian that I thought you could have used. It might have taken the scene in a different direction, but that's what acting's all about. Being aware of the here and now and willing to go anywhere. It means being alert to yourself and all that's happening. I think there's still some distance for you to go on that front. What do you think?"

Her piece said, Sophie looks away to scowl at the seagulls swooping by in search of food.

Gabriella reflects on all she's heard. "Everything I do on stage," she starts. "Everything's instinctive…"

"Which is great, don't get me wrong," interrupts Sophie.

"And I'm nervous that if I step back and examine it, it'll become unnatural," concludes Gabriella.

Sophie leans towards her. "How can you get better if you don't know what you're doing? Not once but always? Constantly?"

Gabriella shuffles on the bench. She stretches her good left leg out and rotates her ankle.

"That must feel good," relents Sophie.

Gabriella nods absent-mindedly and then, as if getting a weight off her chest, "I've been sort of offered a part. In a new soap. Not a lead but it's the BBC and… After the play, this agent Antoine…"

"Antoine Jabeur? That little, self-important Napoleon of a man?"

Gabrielle nods, "He is on the short side, you're right, but that's not the thing. The thing is, this part, which he says all I need to do is meet the director and I've got it, this part would mean having to quit the school… And I don't know what to do."

Gabriella brings her eyes to Sophie's and frowns. Her mentor's not looking as fantastically overwhelmed with glee as she'd thought she'd be.

Sophie lights another cigarette and marshals her thoughts. Finally, "Look, I'm truly pleased for you that Antoine's got something for you. Even if it is a small part in a soap. It's good to see your talent's being recognised… But I need to ask, do you think you're ready for it?"

Gabriella feels the tears coming to her eyes and takes a long breath to compose herself. "I thought I was, but after all you've just said…"

Sophie can't help pointing out, "There's a really big ocean out there of really talented, really unemployed actors. The ones who fully make it are the ones who build off a solid foundation by constantly honing and improving their skills. It's a true craft."

Gabriella nods her understanding, not daring herself to speak.

"And so," continues Sophie more softly now, "my real question for you is simply...do you see yourself in art or do you see the art in yourself?"

Gabriella leans over the side of the cot to pick Harmony up. On days like today - most days in fact - holding her daughter in her arms is the whole world to her.

She looks at her girl and draws back a lock of hair from her face. "Do you know what Mummy's just done, my little precious? Mummy's just fired the one and only agent she's ever had. Oh yes, she did. Silly Mummy, eh? What does my angel think about that?"

And Harmony beams in approval.

Self-Reflection

1. Is there anything you do which feels for you like acting feels for Gabriella?
2. What truly drives you with the skills you have – recognition by others or greater expertise?
3. Is there anything you do which you are both passionate about and great at?
4. How do you know you're great at it?

11. Kieran Has A Word

The TV screen flickers in the darkness. Mifune strides down the village high street from one camp to another. How will he play them off against each other this time? Yojimbo. One of Kurosawa's finest samurai dramas and the inspiration for Leone's A Fistful of Dollars. Kieran has seen it dozens of times.

It's past 3am on an early Tuesday morning in October. Gabriella and Harmony are fast asleep upstairs but insomnia has long been part of Kieran's life. It was on a night like tonight, a few years ago, that Kieran once called the Samaritans. Unlike Kurosawa himself, he didn't have a planned intention as such, but he realised he did need to speak to someone. It was after Silvia had left him, and the depression that had also been part of his life for a long time wouldn't lift.

Kieran has never blamed his wife for leaving the marriage. She fell in love with someone else and moved out. She was true to herself and to him. She never pretended otherwise. They'd had a remarkably amicable divorce and had kept in touch, not just for the kids but for themselves as well. Growing apart had not meant going their separate ways too.

Yet the black river which had bubbled underneath for years had risen, and one by one, Kieran had closed the doors and withdrawn. That phonecall had pulled Kieran back from the brink and had started him opening the doors again.

Tonight's not on that level. Kieran's not depressed, just a little lost. This book he's trying to deliver is refusing to be conceived let alone born. Silvia's task for him is to find his voice, yet one bright idea after another has led inexorably to a dead-end. Last week he'd shown to a friend a couple of chapters he'd written for a planned 'lightly comic' book about auditing. The friend had been such a good friend that he'd left Kieran in no uncertain terms as to how awful the concept was. It's good to know he has people who feel they can say that to him, but it still drops him back at square one.

Kieran watches Mifune chuckle to himself at the greed of the villagers. The plot is minimal, the lessons for us all huge. How do the masters make it look so easy?

Harmony's doing her best not to live up to her name today. One cherished toy follows another out of the pushchair as they amble through the park. Passing mothers cluck and smile indulgently at Grandad's troubles and hurry on thankfully.

Kieran and Harmony have watched the swans. They have been to the playground. They have largely avoided the prying wet noses of dogs. They – Grandad – have had a very strong coffee. Mood-wise, not much is working.

As Kieran pushes his granddaughter up an incline, a voice suddenly calls out beside him, "Waahey! I thought it was you!" It's Connor, a bright kid from his old team. "I see retirement's done wonders for you," he jokes.

As Harmony chucks her bear with impressive accuracy and force at the young man, Kieran pauses to scan the overcast skies. "Hmm, not sure I've retired. Is that what they're saying?", he asks.

"They're actually calling it 'doing a Kieran'," replies Connor with a noticeable level of awe in his tone. "Standing up and walking out. Half the team have gone in the last month. Between you and me, not sure I won't either. The takeover's not been strawberries and cream at all. Wouldn't be surprised if we see the back of Mark too one day soon."

"I'm sorry to hear that," responds Kieran, genuinely concerned for his former colleagues.

"Don't be," says Connor. "Truth is, we all saw you as a bit of a hero, a rebel. You showed us the way."

Kieran sighs. "You know, what worked for me might not work for others. Might not work for you even. You're smart and well regarded. There'll be some really good opportunities ahead with the bigger scope Vortex have brought in. You could go far if you stayed on. If your heart's in it, that is." He studies the younger man's unmistakably deflated face, which seems to be saying Kieran has just royally rained on his parade. "Fact of the matter is," continues Kieran. "In my own unique, particular case, I wasn't really cut out to be a CFO. I mean, sure, it had its moments, but I just kind of fell into it. Growing up, all my heroes, all the people I looked up to were in very different fields... I was... I was in therapy for years... I can see that's quite a surprise to you."

"You were always so…cheerful in the office…larking around," stammers Connor.

"Sometimes we need to look beyond the mask… Sorry, that sounds a tad self-righteous. I don't mean to be. Anyway, my advice to you would be to hold your horses for the time being. Think of the longer term." And with that, Kieran beams at his old team member.

Connor shrugs noncommittally. "Be seeing you around, I guess." He stoops to pick up and gingerly return Harmony's bear. With a half-nod and smile, he wanders off in the other direction.

Kieran watches him go and then turns to his granddaughter. "And that, my beautiful young princess, just illustrated how advice is always such a waste of breath for everyone concerned."

Harmony blows an exceptionally loud raspberry at him.

It's a wet Wednesday night late in October and it's a cup match. Inverness CT. And it's been as woeful as only cup matches on wet Wednesday nights in October can be. The one saving grace so far that anyone in the Wheatfield Stand around Kieran can identify is that at least it's not January. That Hearts are actually winning 1-0 seems irrelevant. It's woeful.

Kieran looks at the guys alongside him, and notes as always that yes, it's all guys. Season ticket holders like himself. Here, rain or shine, week in week out, season after season. He knows them all by first name only, has seen their sons come and go and then join the group later, has remarked on occasional absences and sometimes new faces taking their places. Thankfully, the game's changing. More women and families are coming along these days, but this section of the stand seems to remain unmoved. They sit next to each other, swap jokes and stories and pies, insult the ref, argue the merits of the new signings, celebrate the goals and wins, and commiserate the losses all together. And come the final whistle, each and every one of them disappears back into his own life without a moment's hesitation. Kieran thinks back to his father and his grandfather, and then to his own boys, Mauricio and David. He looks at all the men around him and grasps just how little he knows what's really going on in their heads.

And there, as clearly as if the clouds have parted and Silvia has reached down to box him on the ears, comes the idea for his book. Oblivious to whatever's happening on the pitch, Kieran stands up and starts to shuffle his way along the row of seats to the aisle. Behind him, to a roar of laughter, someone shouts, "Where ye off to, Kieran? Aye, it may be parlous, yet it'll be the same next week, and the week after that too, you know it."

But he's gone.

Kieran looks across at his old friend Mark as they clink their glasses. "I bumped into Connor recently and it made me realise I hadn't seen you for the longest while. I've been too caught up in my own little world. How's it all going?"

Mark wipes his top lip and settles back into their booth. It's a pub over by the Meadows, one of their old haunts from when they were at uni together. "Aye, not too bad," he offers less than convincingly. "That Connor'll be the death of me. Had to have a wee heart to heart with him about life and the universe and all. He was grilling me on my vision for the company. Purpose and all that," exhales Mark. "I was nervous about losing him, but I think he's coming round to the new direction with Vortex."

"I was asking about you," reminds Kieran gently.

Mark eyes him and gives in. "Well, I've had better years to be honest. But I've made my decision and it's all good. Six months and then it's the golf club and Mrs McRae and her never-ending complaints about members blocking her drive."

"Cheers to that," toasts Kieran.

"Aye, thanks. No doubt I'll be banging on the door soon enough begging to be let back," smiles Mark.

"Somehow I doubt that. Your handicap's still...what was the word I heard the other day? Parlous... Good word for a writer, that," muses Kieran before laughing as Mark frowns nervously. "Don't worry, I'm not going to ask you to read anything."

"Thank Jesus for that," exclaims Mark more strongly than he'd intended. "Sorry, no offence meant."

"And none taken," grins Kieran before adding, "but I do have an idea, a good one this time."

Ever the loyal friend, Mark looks at him expectantly. "And?"

"I'm going to write about depression. And about being a man and how we deal with it. Or not, as the case might be. How there are truths and depths we avoid as men. How we hide from ourselves as much as we hide from others."

Mark notes the change that comes over Kieran as he talks. He looks his friend in the eye. "Finally I hear your heart talking. That is one book I would like to read."

Kieran's touched by the genuine sentiment. "Thanks," he breathes, and they hold the silence for a moment.

And then Mark eases the mood. "You should come by the office one day. God knows why but they appear to really miss you." He glances at his beer and then away at the passing barmaid.

Kieran tilts his pint at the dig and drinks. As he does so, he reflects for his book how this teasing banter is how guys show each other affection. Good or bad, it's simply the way it is.

Kieran promises Mark he will indeed look in one day. It's a promise, so he knows he will do so. He's just not sure when.

The two friends smile and turn to talk of other things as men usually do.

Self-Reflection
1. What keeps you awake at nights?
2. What can you do about this?
3. How receptive are you to others' advice?

4. What do you do when you're looking for inspiration?

12. Jacqui Jumps

It can be very humbling experiencing a nation's bureaucracy from an outsider's perspective. The inexplicable nuances, the labyrinthine approval chain, the endless shuffle from one counter to another, the mysterious taste in hold music... Jacqui would gladly settle for humbling if she could calm herself down sufficiently to stop dreaming of throttling someone.

And yet, here she finally sits with Shamsa, who has remained calm and quietly resolute through every step of the journey leading up to this seat in a loud and busy HIV clinic. Here the Syrian refugee will be seen at last by a specialist and her medication programme planned out.

From a sense of outrage if nothing else, Jacqui has repeatedly tried to recount the horrific circumstances of how Shamsa became infected, but the latter keeps holding a hand out to stop her. "It's enough that they know my condition. No more is necessary." And on this, as with everything else, Shamsa is calm and quietly resolute.

23 years old, her family killed in a government air strike, her body.... Jacqui marvels at the younger woman's fortitude. Shunned by the other refugees for her condition and for the memories it triggers in them, Shamsa had been reluctant to share her story with Jacqui. Yet palliative care nurses can also be tough nuts to crack.

Jacqui reaches out and holds Shamsa's hand for support as her name is called. She can't help wondering who's supporting who.

When we have big things to think, enigmas and riddles to ponder, we all have places we go. For some, it's the mountains and the open spaces. For others, it's a crowded cinema with other lives up on the screen in front. For Jacqui, it's always been a church or a place of worship, whatever the religion.

And so here she sits. In her parents' church on a bright October morning. *The fruit don't fall far from the tree,* as her mother would have said in her strong Trini lilt. A few moments ago, Father Anthony had smiled at her in passing and had known better than to disturb any further.

Jacqui looks around herself at the church of her childhood. It probably wouldn't cross her mind that she's honouring her parents by being here, though she does recognise the serenity the stone walls offer. She puzzles over what Mum and Dad would have thought of the video screen Father Anthony's put in.

Silvia was strong in her dreams again last night. It's been less than a year since her partner died and still the hues and tones of her grief darken and lighten from moment to moment. Ebbing, flowing. Anger, sadness, rage. Raw, needling pain. Jagged tears for hours... And now guilt too. Guilt that Jacqui's recognising she needs to move. That this continued stasis is tearing her apart. She lives in the flat they shared, sleeps in the bed they loved in. Even today she reached out to lay a hand where Silvia used to lie. Working with the refugees is wonderful and meaningful, yet with every step she feels she's walking in someone else's shadow.

Jacqui doesn't want to bury Silvia. She doesn't want to put all her memories of their time together in a box and store it far away. But she does see that she needs a new way forward now. One that is hers. One that Silvia can no longer guide her along.

Jacqui sits and thinks what this path might look like.

"It's killing me, but to break free like you want me to, I need to break free from you as well." Turned to the sea, Jacqui stands in the drizzle on their Gullane beach, the wind licking at the tears on her face. "I see you in everything I do. I hear your voice, I feel your breath, I smell your scent... Everything... Your toothbrush is still... And I know you don't want this for me. I know you want me to go my own way...but I'm terrified I'll lose the little I have left of you. I'm terrified that I won't be the person you loved any more..."

Jacqui breaks off and folds into herself as a gust throws spume off the sea at her. She cocks her head to one side to listen to the sky for some kind of response.

Silence.

Calmer now, "And I don't want to be that bitter old woman in the corner of the pub moaning about the world. It's not who I am, and yet I've lost my....tolerance, my patience. I don't know the right word. And I'm spending so much time at the centre trying to keep you alive that they're sick of me... But it's not just you and us. It's me too... I'm sorry. I'm rambling. I can't do bullet points like you. But you get my drift, yeah?" Jacqui giggles despite herself. "A sign of some nature would go down really well right about now. Can't you do that at least?"

Jacqui stretches her arms wide and stands waiting.

Again, silence.

"So be it. Don't blame me if I go off the rails and go and become a nun or something. You had your chance," she scolds her lost love fondly.

Still smiling, Jacqui turns back from the sea. The rain has relented, and in the distance a couple of young women are sitting on their coats on the sand. Seeing them trying to lay out a picnic in the still driving wind, Jacqui can't help thinking to herself, *They're brave.* And as if with that thought, a seagull dives in and snatches a sandwich off the top of one of their bags. The girls shriek with surprise and then roll over, squealing with laughter.

Jacqui smiles even wider. It's their beach now.

Jacqui looks at her room and wonders how she's meant to move in it. Her bed is a thin metal cot with an even thinner mattress. Her bag just fits under it. On both walls – which she can touch with her outstretched hands – a single row of wooden planks serves as shelving. There's a dusty window, a small mirror at the end of her bed, and an old bare chair. She decides she'll work out what to use that for later.

Jacqui comes back out onto the open landing. The Himalayas rise high and majestic all around her, the Annapurna range on one side of the deep ravine, Dhaulagiri on the other. A thin and tired mule leads a small boy on a rope along a lane nearby. She watches him stop and talk to an old woman sitting on a tall coil of plastic tubing before the mule pulls him on again.

Jomsom's a short plane ride up from Pokhara, yet not a flight Jacqui and her stomach will forget in a hurry. With a population of just over a thousand, it's not exactly Easter Road, but it's certainly busier than some of the villages she's been through. At 2700 metres above sea level, the town's the gateway to the Mustang region and will be her home for the next year.

Jacqui can't help feeling inordinately proud of herself. *When I jump, I really do jump*, she grins to the late afternoon sky. From seeing the ad for an immediate opening in Nepal with Médecins Sans Frontières to getting here has taken less than a month. She's taken a sabbatical from the NHS, put her flat up for rent with an agency, said goodbye to her counsellor, wished her refugee friends well, and given half of her wardrobe to Father Anthony for the homeless. The rest she's wearing right now or at least it feels that way. She'd been warned about the winds racing up the valley in the afternoons.

The ad had ticked all the boxes. Jacqui had known her only way forward was a significant step into the unknown. Once she got to the very lip of that step, she realised she just had to close her eyes and fall forward. Otherwise she'd still be in Edinburgh now, humming and hawing. She kissed herself over the edge and now here she is. *What would Silvia have thought?*, she chortles to herself.

A month later and Jacqui's hiked up to Kagbeni, a small village three hours on foot north of Jomsom. She could have got a lift with someone, but she had some time and it seemed sacrilegious not to walk this leg of the Annapurna circuit. She's going to spend a couple of days here helping the local doctor before they go on together to Muktinath, another village on the circuit and a Hindu pilgrimage site. Her work so far in Nepal has been intense. The resources available are not what she's used to, nor are the conditions she sees in her patients. Chronic illnesses untreated for years, simple fractures and wounds worsened by the distance and time taken to get to help, the stark realities of poverty expressed in innumerable ways. If she'd wanted a leap into a different world, she's certainly got it.

And now she sits with an apprentice nun from the Tharwa Chyoling Nunnery, a woman probably her age but with her life etched in deep lines across her face. The woman is dying of lung cancer and knows it. *Smoking*, she'd offered with a shrug earlier, a mischievous gleam in her heavy-lidded eyes. Her English is good and Jacqui's curious as to how she's only an apprentice at her age.

"A big landslide last year. Took my family, my house, all," the woman offers simply.

Jacqui eyes her in wonder.

The nun studies her reaction and pats her hand consolingly. And then a thought comes to her and she leans in, "A farmer has a great horse. It wins a prize in a competition. His neighbour comes and congratulates him. The farmer answers, 'Who knows what's good and what's bad?'"

The woman looks at Jacqui out of the corner of her eye. "You have a cigarette?" Jacqui laughs and shakes her head. With the smallest of scowls, she continues, "The horse is stolen by thieves and this time the neighbour comes to say sorry. Again the farmer says, 'Who knows what's good and what's bad?' The horse escapes and leads the other horses the thieves have to the farmer. The neighbour sees all the horses and smiles, 'Who knows what's good and what's bad?'"

The woman coughs a tearing, rasping rattle of a cough. She composes herself and takes up her story again, a little more softly this time. "The farmer's son goes to ride this great horse, but he falls off and breaks his leg. Who knows, etc, etc. And the next day, the army comes through the village taking all the boys into the army. But they don't take the farmer's son because of his leg. And the farmer thinks to himself, 'Who knows what's good and what's bad?'"

The woman leans back, grins at Jacqui, and looks to the mountains. And in this moment, just maybe, Jacqui starts to find some peace in herself.

Self-Reflection
1. What tough decisions have you had to make to get where you are today?
2. What have you had to give up along the way?
3. How do you 'kiss yourself over the edge' with an important yet daunting change?
4. How do you celebrate your successes?

13. Ignacio Finds A Way

Ignacio finds himself thinking in hands these days. One hand surgery back in his consultancy will give them so much diesel for the bus. Two hand surgeries will feed the kids for so long. And so it goes. He's never really thought in such coldly monetary terms before and yet he's finding it strangely grounding, purposeful even.

It's coming to the end of his second stay at the orphanage in Havana. The two weeks have flown by, just as they did the first time round. Soon he'll be back in Edinburgh doing again what he's best at. Today though, he's manhandling the bus along some very potholed roads to the beach. The commotion behind him in the bus is something to behold. He's never had to deal with so many kids at once.

In the mirror above him, he rolls his eyes at Lucía sitting behind. She grins back. "You offered," she shouts above the noise. He nods sheepishly, pulling at the wheel to avoid a stray chicken. The children, thirty or so of them, range from five to 12. The younger ones have been left in the care of others back at the orphanage. There aren't any children over 12 under their protection. Once anyone gets to that age they're considered old enough to fend for themselves or are picked up by other institutions if they're fortunate.

The bus hits a bump and the kids protest merrily. One of the older ones makes a comment about the driver looking more at the *doctora* than at the road and they all laugh and catcall. This is going to be one long, long day, reflects Ignacio to himself.

"How are you doing?", asks Lucía with a gentle smile as she comes out into the night air later the same day.

Ignacio's sitting on the balcony, his arms resting on the railings as he watches the late evening bustle in the street below. "Fine," he tries. "Liar. You're exhausted, look at you." She kisses him on the top of his head as she sits down beside him. "That was kind of you today, thank you." She nestles into him, lays her head on his arm to look down as he does.

"They're good kids," he says.

Lucía prods him in the ribs. "All of them?", she laughs.

"Yeah, well, they're kids..."

They sit in silence for a while. And then Lucía quietly asks, "What are you doing here?"

Ignacio exhales. "I was two when my father disappeared. Silvia had some memories of him but me, nothing. I'm not comparing myself to what these guys have gone through but..." He drifts off, lost in his thoughts.

"All the things you do...They love you already."

"Really?" This seems to come as some surprise to him. "All of them?", he jokes.

"Yeah, well, they're kids...", she teases back.

They laugh and then the silence returns. Two small ants chase each other along the railing.

Eventually, Ignacio says, "I'm concerned about Álvaro. He's bright but he hangs back. I think the other kids pick on him. He didn't get involved in any of the games today."

"Hmmm, yes, I've noticed that too... He does well in his classes. I'm trying to see if we can get some kind of grant or scholarship or anything to help him. Education's the only way out for these children but all too often it comes down to just surviving," Lucía explains. "When smart ones like him have to drop out of school it's such a waste."

"He was asking me about my work, about what it's like being a surgeon, and about anaesthetics and so on. Some sharp questions for a kid his age." Ignacio looks at Lucía and then away again. A group of drunk Canadian tourists pass by underneath, shouting and laughing into the Havana night.

"You got everything for the flight tomorrow?", Lucía asks.

Ignacio nods. "Not looking forward to the cold again."

After another long moment of silence, Lucía pushes softly, "You didn't really answer my earlier question."

"No, I didn't, did I?" Ignacio laughs and makes no attempt to answer it this time either.

Lucía pokes him once more and they kiss.

Flying high above the Atlantic, Ignacio looks back at the last two weeks. For the first time in his life he feels guilty about his business class ticket, something he always used to consider a deserved reward for all he puts into his job.

Up to now, fixing people's hands has been how Ignacio's contributed. Sure, the personal benefits have been great, yet truthfully, the expensive toys and holidays have not been what drives him. Not that he would ever boast about it or frame it to others in this way, but he's seen his work as a kind of mission, as his own unique way of helping people to the best of his ability. Silvia had her teaching and her refugees and her own kids. He has his hands and his medical expertise. Their mother instilled in them both this sense of service. Now, as he sits back in the dimly lit cabin, his fellow passengers all asleep or lost in their video screens, he wonders if there may be other ways he can heal the world now.

"What would you do?" Ignacio looks at the ten-year-old boy sitting alongside him on the dry grass.

Álvaro ponders the scenario and then muses, "I'd check the guy who's not screaming. The woman who's screaming, she's got the energy to scream and is alert. The guy who's just lying there, he may be really badly hurt."

Ignacio beams, "Correct answer." And he high-fives the boy. As he does so, he can't help noticing the bruise on his upper arm.

Álvaro catches his look and unconvincingly offers, "I fell." He returns to the book on his lap, one of several Ignacio's brought back with him from Edinburgh this time.

Ignacio frowns and glances over at the other kids playing football. He wonders what he can do to help the situation. Reflecting that Lucía's far more experienced with children than he is, he decides to consult her later.

"So, Álvaro," he starts. "You seem to really like medicine, don't you?"

Álvaro grins up at him, nodding. "These books are really cool, thank you."

"Think you'd like to be a doctor one day?"

Engrossed in the book, Álvaro replies without looking up, "Yeah, but…" His shrug seems to capture how much of a fantasy this would be.

"How about if I tell you that I've got some people together and we're going to help you?", says Ignacio quietly, though his pulse is racing. He puts out of his mind how he has twisted arms and pressganged several of his surgeon colleagues into coming on board with this project over the last month.

"You would?" Álvaro gazes at him with genuine delight. "As in teach me?"

"Well, maybe… But that would come later. And it would depend on what you specialise in. If that's where you go. Because you've got to study maths and science and probably English too. Lots of things. And maybe something will come up along the way that you become more interested in…" Ignacio breaks off to study the boy's reaction.

As with everything else, Álvaro is careful. He thinks it over for a moment. "No, a doctor is what I want to be," he pronounces very seriously.

"Good," says Ignacio, clapping him on the back. "Your government's got lots of schemes later on to help with university and so on, but we're going to help you get there over the next few years. How does that sound?"

"Brilliant," Álvaro smiles up at him in gratitude. He starts to say something else but is interrupted by a football striking him on the knee.

The two look over to see the other boys all standing waiting for them to kick the ball back. "Álvaro! Álvaro!", they start chanting good-naturedly.

Álvaro gets to his feet and kicks the ball hard and deep onto the pitch. The boys cheer and continue roaring, "Álvaro! Álvaro!" They beckon him to come over and play.

Álvaro looks round at Ignacio, who nods and smiles. Seeing their friend left on his own, the kids take up a new chant, "Ignacio! Ignacio! Ignacio!"

Ignacio grins and jumps to his feet too.

Self-Reflection
1. What did you want to be when you were a child?
2. How has your education helped you?

3. What do you do in the service of others?
4. What else could you do?

14. Mauricio Gets The Ball Rolling

Mauricio looks round the room and wonders yet again how it has come to this. 32 years old and living back at home with his father. And what's even worse is that he's babysitting. His father has ensconced himself in his study to write while his sister's out doing the drama queen thing. Leaving him home alone with his dear sweet niece.

Harmony and uncle eye each other across the kitchen table. At our most generous, we could say that trust has yet to develop in this breakfast team. Team member A – Harmony – has just opened proceedings by flicking a spoonful of strawberry yoghurt with unerring aim at the freshly ironed white shirt of team member B – Mauricio. Team member B has responded by removing the bowl of yoghurt and placing it in the middle of the table out of team member A's reach. Both are now glaring at each other across said bowl. Eventually, Mauricio realises he's in a game of wits with a two-year-old. A game, as he can now see, he's losing as Harmony yawns pointedly and turns her attention to picking her nose. Mauricio pushes the bowl back towards her and goes to get another coffee. When he lost his consulting job, Mauricio gave up his flat in London and moved back north to regroup. He'd joked with his family that he was resting, but Gabriella had coolly informed him that the term only applied in the theatrical world. What he was was unemployed, she told him point-blank. His father had been little better, telling him to stay clear of his whisky collection and muttering about zoos and Piccadilly Circus.

Surround yourself with love, his mother had instructed. Is this what she meant?

Mauricio looks around another room and wonders how it has come to this too. Henry the solicitor, of all people, had suggested he give AA a try. Apparently, it had helped him at a certain stage in his life. Mauricio's not convinced he's an alcoholic, not really convinced he has a problem at all in fact, though he does recognise he's on the slippery slope to it becoming one. And so here he finds himself on a wet November evening among a group of around twenty strangers. A group of strangers he can't help finding fascinating. He debates which three demographic criteria would be the primary discriminators. Probably age, ethnicity, and economic status. The next tier down would be a subset of sexual orientation, gender identification, employment status, and marital status. Actually, the list is endless, he reflects, as the most striking aspect so far has been everyone's normality. He was expecting freaks and shouters, but all he's seen so far is a fair cross-section of society. Everyone's calmly drinking tea or coffee or sipping from their own flasks of water. He's seen edgier behaviour at book festival readings his father's dragged him to.

A woman in her forties claps her hands just once and everyone settles into their chairs. With a warm and welcoming smile, she scans them all one by one, and the meeting begins.

Mauricio's not too sure how he ended up here on a park bench in Inverleith. He'd met up with some guys from school he hadn't seen for years, gone for a drink with them, and then had carried on after they left to go home to their families. His own home's not too far away, so maybe he'd just sat down for a bit on the way back. He looks at his watch, catches that it's 11 something as his arm passes by his face, and slumps forward again.

"You alright there, pal?"

"Huh?", Mauricio looks up and tries to focus on the man in front of him. "Yeah, yeah, all good. Cheers."

"Mind if I take a pew there?"

"No, no, free world and all that. Fill your boots." Mauricio gestures expansively at the space next to him on the bench. "Hey, I know you. You're...." His memory fails him again.

"Yup, I'm Jack. We met the other day. At AA." Jack is about Mauricio's age, shaven-headed, and with a big dagger tattoo on his neck.

"That's right. You sell the Big Issue."

"Aye, I do... Tell me, do you live near here?"

"Yeah," Mauricio waves vaguely behind him. "So, Jack, when you're selling the Big Issue, who's your target market?"

Jack laughs. "For real?" He looks around them, notes a group of young guys standing smoking and quietly talking among themselves over by some trees. "I don't really have one, I reckon... Listen, let's get you home, eh?" He stands up and turns to see if Mauricio needs help getting up.

"Big mistake. You've got to know your customer base. Oops." The momentum from Mauricio launching himself to his feet carries him forward several stumbling steps before he crumples to the ground. "Oops," he repeats, giggling.

"Come on then." Jack reaches a hand down to him. "So, which direction are we headed?"

Mauricio lets himself be pulled to his feet. He stands next to Jack, looks around him, and wonders.

"How are you doing, son?" Kieran looks at his eldest child.

"Didn't realise I was so out of shape," replies Mauricio, wiping the sweat off his face.

"Fancy another game? We can call it the decider," offers Kieran, conscious they've still got the squash court booked for another fifteen minutes.

"No, you'll just give it to me. Like you did that last one, didn't you?" Mauricio glares at his father accusingly.

Kieran smiles. "I may indeed have gone easy on a couple of serves. Just this once."

"Well, don't. I'll manage." It comes out harder than intended. "Sorry, Dad. I know I'm being a pain to you all."

Kieran eyes him. "You know, when I was going through therapy, I was told *move, make, meet*. So, exercise or walk or similar, create something, or meet somebody. It really helped with my depression."

"You were in therapy?" Mauricio looks at his father, stunned. "When? You've always been so..."

"Seems we all have our secrets, eh?" Kieran smiles softly.

Mauricio nods back at him. "Seems so... OK then, one more, but if I catch you holding back, you're doing star jumps."

"You do know squash is renowned for giving people my age heart attacks?"

"Stop your blethering, old man," grins Mauricio.

Mauricio, Kieran, and Gabriella all eye each other around the kitchen table more than a little self-consciously. Calling a family meeting like this is not really how they operate. Mauricio, who has initiated the gathering, clears his throat.

"Dad, Sis. Thanks. I know this is... Well, I'm just going to say it. Truth is, I've been a complete arse for quite a while now. I'm sorry it's taken me so long to realise just how much." Mauricio catches his sister's worried glance at their father. "Don't worry, Gabi. I'm not about to top myself. Quite the opposite in fact. In fact... So, several things. First..."

Gabriella rolls her eyes, jokes, "Please, not the list of three again."
Mauricio laughs. "It's how I think. I can't help it... First up is that I'm
moving out."
"Yay!", cheers Gabriella.
"There is a god in heaven," exclaims Kieran, grinning.
"Not the reaction I was wholly hoping for," retorts Mauricio,
beaming.
"All from a place of love, son. All from love," promises his father.
Mauricio looks at him and for a moment is silent. "And I love you too,
Dad."
Gabriella looks at her brother in surprise. She's never heard him say
this to anyone before. "Now I am worried," she says.
Mauricio turns to her and smiles. "And yes, I love you as well, little
sister."
Gabriella is immediately all waterworks. She jumps up and pulls her
brother into her arms. "You old softie," is all she manages.
After a long while, Mauricio helps her back to her chair and wipes his
own eyes. "Second thing...," he continues. "Second thing is that I'm
going to set up my own consultancy. Here in Edinburgh. Cleantech. I
won't bore you with the details now, but cleantech and local
customers. Very small to start with. I've got a few contacts and leads.
I'm sure you can open some doors too, Dad."
"Aye, that I can, Mauricio. Well done, I'm proud of you," says Kieran.
"We both are," adds Gabriella, threatening to burst into tears again.
"And the third thing...," Mauricio breaks off for the longest ten
seconds of his life. He studies them both and finds courage from
somewhere. "Someone once said that looking into a human being is

like looking into an abyss. There are so many truths and secrets and stories swirling around in us. It's like chaos. And right now, I'm fully in this abyss and you're both like a vine hanging down to help me out. I need your help, please."

And with this both Kieran and Gabriella grab Mauricio for the best hug he's ever had.

"I'll take one of those, please."

Jack looks up and recognises Mauricio. "No free handouts. That'll be three quid. I've got one of them fancy card machines if you need."

"No free handouts," agrees Mauricio. He reaches into his pocket for some coins. "Anything worth reading this week?", he asks as Jack hands him a magazine.

"Good interview with Michael Sheen and the stuff he does for the homeless community in Wales," says Jack, squinting against the winter sun. He's at his regular pitch outside a Sainsbury's.

"Ever see him in Good Omens with our own Dave Tennant?", asks Mauricio.

"Brilliant, eh?"

"Indeed," agrees Mauricio. "You got a moment?"

Jack eyes him and nods. The two walk off a short distance to sit on a low wall. "What's up, brother?"

"I've just moved into a new place. All on my own. And it's got a spare room." Mauricio turns to his friend. "I was wondering if it might work for you. You know, until things..." He drifts off.

"That'd be grand. But I'd want to pay you for it." Jack holds his finger up. "No free handouts, like I said."

Mauricio nods. "How about paying me in kind? No rent. Bills we can talk about, but maybe you do some work for me?"

"Like what?", asks Jack, intrigued as to how he could help.

"I've got a project in mind, and I need someone to bounce ideas off. Someone I can talk things through with. But more importantly, I need someone to tell it to me straight. Not to pussyfoot or turn a blind eye. Someone who's going to keep me honest and hold me to account."

Jack scratches the stubble on his chin. After a long moment, he nods. "OK, but you've got to do one thing for me first."

Mauricio gets to his feet and looks around the room. He smiles as he realises this isn't as difficult as he'd thought it be.

"Evening. My name's Mauricio and I'm an alcoholic."

Self-Reflection
1. Do you have someone in your life who supports you unconditionally?
2. Do you have someone in your life who tells it to you straight?
3. If not in either case, who could you ask?
4. How could they hold you to account?

15. Henry Sets A Direction

There are 282 Munros in Scotland. Climbing them all is like scaling Mount Everest 17 times or walking from Edinburgh to Greece in distance terms. Bagging the 282 is many a mountaineer's dream even if there are few that are truly demanding technically. Henry's on 231, so he's close to getting there. He just wishes the remaining 51 didn't include the 11 Cuillin Munros on the Isle of Skye, especially the notorious and notoriously named Inaccessible Pinnacle.

Henry sits in his office and reluctantly pulls his mind back from the dreams of peaks far away. An email flashes up on his screen, notifying him that someone's just made a transfer into Ignacio's educational trust fund. Henry checks the account and whistles. A healthy transfer at that. Henry was humbled to be asked by Ignacio to administer the trust he's set up for the orphans. At the moment, they're focussing on the kids in Lucía's orphanage, yet Ignacio's already making noises about taking it wider to the whole of Latin America in time.

It's getting close to when the tribe will meet up again. Henry wonders if they'll all have honoured Silvia's wishes and lived up to the tasks she set them. He looks at the grey cowbell on his desk and smiles in recollection of all the comments he's had about it. It's 5.30pm and time to close the office for the day. He can't resist picking the bell up and giving it a quick ring. What would his wife Isabel have said if she could see him now, ringing a cowbell to mark the end of a day's work?

As he places the bell carefully back on the corner of his desk, Henry's phone pings in his breast pocket with a missed call. Against his better judgment, he pulls it out and checks who's calling him at this time of the day. He frowns at seeing his daughter Josie's name. For a moment he feels guilty about this, and then realises this doesn't help anyone. Eat the frog, as he was once told. Don't dither and put off what needs to be done. He hits the call back button.

"Now then, I understand you're thinking of joining our rescue team?" The man sitting across from Henry is half his age, twice as hairy, and three times his size. How he fits through the room's low doorway is anyone's guess. Maybe they airlift him out through the roof like in Thunderbirds, considers Henry and he fights to stifle a giggle. Working in his own legal practice all his career means Henry's never interviewed for a job before. Understandably perhaps, he's somewhat nervous.

The man – Calum – regards him expectantly.

Henry nods and marshals his thoughts more appropriately. "Look, I'm 64, so I'm sure you probably think I'm too old. But I've been in the mountains in some form or another all my life. The Cairngorms in particular."

Henry studies Calum to see how this lands before continuing. "I'm about to retire, though I haven't told anyone yet." He's amazed to hear himself utter these words to a complete stranger. *Are all interviews like going to confession*?, he wonders. "The work you guys do is important, purposeful even. I've never been unfortunate enough to have to call you out myself, but I know people who have."

"Maybe you've planned and prepared better than others," offers Calum.

"That's kind of you, but we both know bad things can happen to anyone. My father was killed on Annapurna, and the only thing he ever planned for was the mountains."

"I'm sorry to hear," says Calum, watching him with keener interest now.

"I'm fit and healthy. Still have all my own teeth," jokes Henry, feeling more and more comfortable. "Seriously, I understand my age works against me, but if there's a role I can fulfil, whatever it is, I'm your man. I leave it totally up to you to decide how I can help."

Calum studies him before taking up in one of his massive paws the piece of paper on the table between them. "It says on your application that you live in Edinburgh. That's a wee distance for us to call you out of a night."

"I'm moving up here fulltime. Still looking for a place but likely either Newtonmore or Kingussie. I'm not a fan of Aviemore, I'm afraid. My place in the city's already on the market." Again, Henry is surprised to be telling Calum all this. Not even Josie knows yet.

"Kincraig or somewhere like that would be even better for us, but your call. Our volunteers have usually got a four-wheel drive and can get to us within half an hour whatever the conditions," replies Calum calmly.

Henry nods his understanding.

"Got any medical training?", asks Calum.

"First Aid certificates renewed every three years. That's it on that front. Otherwise, taught navigation and winter walking skills to kids for a while back when my daughter was younger. Been up most of the summits in the Cairngorms. Some of them multiple times. Oh yes, and National Ice Water Swimming Champion 1978," smiles Henry.

Calum shudders, "I hope you'll never have to use that one." He sits back in his plastic chair, which is threatening to buckle at any moment under his weight. "When you're up here and settled in, come and talk to me again. I'll see what we can do for each other," he promises.

Henry nods and gets to his feet just as Calum's chair does indeed buckle with a crash. He looks down at the sprawled figure on the ground. "Is this part of the interview?"

It's a crisp winter day. Sun in the sky, snow on the ground. Henry is walking with Josie in the Pentlands, a row of hills just to the south of Edinburgh. It would be a fine day were it not for the fact that Josie's brought her little yappy dog Sam along with her, something she knows will irritate her father. For Henry, Sam represents yet another element in his daughter's life which she inexplicably loves against all logic and reason, a category which includes as far as he's concerned her husband Paul and the area of Penicuik where they live.

Sam is with them as Josie is keen to express her ongoing disappointment in Henry opting out of Hogmanay with Paul and her to swan off to Cuba for a jolly. For his part, Henry still thinks it such a good excuse that he might well use it again next year. The simple truth that he chose to visit the orphanage which is now taking up so much of his time – unbilled – seems to be irrelevant in the current family dynamics.

They walk in silence, their feet scrunching on the snow. Still, Josie has expressed her displeasure and knows it has been registered by her father. It's too good a day to waste in rubbing the salt in further.

"What was it like over there?", she asks generously.

Henry stops to reflect. "Both inspiring and heart-breaking. They're facing a lot of challenges. But they're dedicated. Some amazing people. And the kids are resilient for the most part."

"And the investment from the trust? Is it sizeable?", Josie asks, intrigued.

"For now, it's plenty... But Ignacio's got big plans. He's set out a number of milestones he wants to achieve. It's ambitious in my view, but he's got some real commitment and direction from the trustees. There's a proper plan in place. I'm impressed," Henry replies.

"I hear respect and maybe a wee bit of pride too," Josie teases her father.

"It's good to be doing something worthwhile. It's the one portfolio I'm going to keep running," says Henry without thinking.

Josie halts in her tracks. "What do you mean, Dad?"

"Ah, yes. That." Henry stops and turns to face her. "I meant to tell you earlier... No, that's not true. I might have been avoiding it." He makes a guilty face before looking out over Edinburgh gleaming in the sun, and then back to his daughter. "I've made a couple of decisions... I'm retiring next month. The other partners are going to buy me out." He smiles at Josie.

"Well, that I'm pleased to hear about, I think. But now I'm wondering... What are you going to do with all your time? You're still young," she points out.

Henry can't help reaching a hand out to pat his child. "You're just like your Ma. Always worrying about me. I'll be fine," he says gently.

"I'm serious, Dad. You don't do lazing at home very well... Crap in fact."

"And I'm moving to Colyumbridge," adds Henry quickly.

"Colyumbridge?! That's miles away! Out in the middle of nowhere."

"You know how much I love the Cairngorms. I'll have loads of walks and hills to explore up there... And it's close to the mountain rescue teams if I'm needed." Henry watches her face to see her reaction.

"You're not going to go up in the snow in the middle of night to rescue people at your age, are you?", protests Josie, her expression incredulous. "Have you gone doolally already?"

"I thought you said I was still young," Henry jokes.

"You know what I meant. Really, what is it with people? Does no one ever think about anyone else?" And Josie storms off up the path in front of them, dragging Sam along by his leash. It's the first time Henry has nearly felt sorry for the dog.

By the time he catches up with his daughter, her face is wet with tears. Henry puts his arm around her and leads her over to lean against a boulder. "What is it, Josie?", he asks gingerly.

Josie flings her arms around him and sobs for a moment. After a while, she pulls back and composes herself a little. "I'm sorry, Dad.

I'm happy for you, I really am. You've got it all sussed. It's so great, it really is…. It's just that… You're talking of milestones and commitment and direction… And then I look at myself and I don't have any of that. I don't know what I'm doing or where I'm going. I just am…day in day out…" Josie trails off.

"That's good too, Josie. You don't need to have it all mapped out like I do. You don't need to put pressure on yourself about this. Just so long as you're happy." Henry lets the last sentence hang in the air as he looks at her.

"Oh Dad, it's not that simple. You and your plans. Life's different. Shit happens. Mothers die. Husbands are twats…" Her voice hardens.

"It doesn't all have to be perfect, lass. We can make it up as we go along."

"You going to start singing *Que será, será*?", asks Josie, her tone softening.

Henry laughs. "I wouldn't do that to you. But seriously… Your grandad used to say…"

"Seems like he had a saying for most things," Josie can't help herself.

"Aye, that he did," admits Henry before continuing. "He'd say you can look up and think you've got to the top and then you realise it's just a false summit. And you can either moan that it's just another false summit and you've still got so far to go to the top. Or you can celebrate that it's one more step ticked off and you're that much closer."

"Are you seriously telling me yet another mountain proverb? You know, I might just push you off one of your beloved mountains myself one day," warns Josie.

"I wouldn't do that. I've got a clause in my will that if you're within 50 metres of me when I die, you're getting nothing," grins Henry.

Josie punches him on the arm. "You know what? I believe you. You're that careful."

They lean against the boulder in peaceful silence for a moment.

"You know you can come and stay whenever you want or need to. For as long as you want," says Henry, his gaze still turned towards Edinburgh.

"And if I do, will you help me work out some kind of way forward?"

"Of course. And I've got quite a nice little structure an old friend thought up," says Henry.

"Can I bring Sam?"

"If you bring that sorry little excuse for an animal with you, it may not be me that gets pushed off a hillside."

"Don't worry, I've taken out insurance on him," laughs Josie.

"Good girl," approves Henry.

Self-Reflection

1. How are you with 'eating the frog'? Do you put things off or tackle difficulties at once?
2. How do you feel about retiring one day?
3. What do you do in your life that you will continue doing whatever the challenge?

4. Can you remember all the pieces that go into the structure Henry mentions to Josie?

16. The Tribe Gather Again

As David and Montse get off the coach at Castro, Gabriella's the first to spot them. "There they are," she shrieks and runs over to embrace her brother. Mauricio strolls up behind her to join in the reunion. David introduces them both to Montse and together they make their way out of the bus station to the car park.

As they go, Mauricio can't help joking, "Good to see my little brother's punching above his weight."

Montse blushes as David remarks to his sister, "I thought you said he'd changed?"

"He still has his moments," Gabriella replies with a weary smile as Mauricio laughs.

"Everyone else here?", asks David.

"Yeah, you're the last to arrive. Jacqui got in late last night from Nepal. You should hear her stories. Amazing," says Mauricio.

"And Harmony?", wonders David, suddenly realising his niece is not with them.

"With her great-grandmother. They're inseparable. I think she's making a *machi* out of her," smiles Gabriella.

"I wouldn't put it past her... Look, Montse!", David exclaims as they come to Guillermina's tan Cadillac. Hand in hand, the two gaze at the car fondly. David instinctively turns to Montse and they kiss.

"Hey hey, less of that. This isn't a private limo service, you know," admonishes Mauricio jokingly as he gets into the driver's seat.

Gabriella joins him in front as Montse and David drop their bags in the boot before climbing in the back.

"That thunk just now sounded like a cowbell," says Mauricio as they drive off.

"Yeah, the customs guy was quite taken by it," replies David.

Gabriella catches Montse's eye in the mirror. "We were all sorry to hear about your father."

"Thank you. He had a full life…," smiles Montse before adding, "David says you're going to be a big star."

"*Abuelita* said she was good," nods Gabriella to David in the mirror with a twinkle in her eye.

"Please don't encourage her. Her head's big enough as it is," sighs Mauricio to Montse, for which he's rewarded with a playful slap.

"Are we there yet?", asks David to a chorus of groans.

Henry stands with Kieran, sipping a glass of wine on Guillermina's terrace. "I can see why she wanted to come back," he says looking out towards the mainland where the Andes glitter like burnished gold in the end of day sun. "It's beautiful."

"Aye, she talked about this place a lot," agrees Kieran. "And how there's no midges either!"

"A true blessing."

Kieran watches the solicitor as he gazes at the mountains. "Did your father ever…?"

Henry shakes his head. "They were on his list, but no, events took him a different way."

"It must have been hard to lose him so young," considers Kieran.

"Och, it put responsibilities on me, true. Things I thought I had to do or be for a long time, but I'm my own man these days," smiles Henry.

"And you, now that you're your own man too, how's the writing coming along?"

Kieran shrugs. "Good days and bad. Just like depression really, with all its ebbs and flows. Know any non-depressed writers? There you go, maybe that's an idea I can work into the next draft somehow. Cheers," he grins and clinks his glass with Henry's.

Jacqui comes out to join them in marvelling at the line of peaks in the distance. "Feels like the Himalayas, just wetter." She breathes the evening air deep into her lungs.

"How are you holding up?", asks Kieran.

"So so, I reckon. My body clock's either way ahead of you or far behind. Haven't worked out which yet." The lines around her eyes crease.

"You enjoying it over there?" Henry studies the nurse as the light darkens around them.

Jacqui muses for a while before responding. "Enjoy would be debatable. Certainly not all the time. But challenged, stretched, fulfilled, inspired, awestruck? Yes, all of those."

Henry smiles at her. "It's good to jump, eh?"

Jacqui tilts her glass in agreement and takes a long drink. "How have the kids been?," she asks Kieran.

"They go from being my little babies to more ancient and wiser than I'll ever be and back again all in the same sentence," he replies. "They miss their Mum," he ends softly.

"We all do," she answers simply.

Henry lets the words settle for a while before clearing his throat. "Well, I'd best be off back to the hotel. A long day tomorrow."

"Are we doing our meeting here?", asks Jacqui, finishing off her wine and putting the glass down on a small table.

Henry shakes his head. "Guillermina has rather a surprise for us. I think you'll like it." He winks at them both, nods good night and wanders back inside to take his leave of the others.

Guillermina stands at her sink washing the last of the dinner plates. It's quiet now and the night is full outside. The others have all gone back to their hotel or are nestling down in various corners of her house. Her son Ignacio comes up behind and puts his arms around her. She leans back into his embrace and they stand like that in silence for a moment, looking out into the dark. High above, the sky glistens with stars.

"No parent should have to bury their child," she complains in little more than a whisper.

"Dad would be proud of you. All these years," Ignacio breathes, his chin resting in the white curls on the top of her head.

Guillermina sighs. "That man... I never thought we'd be apart this long." As her son gives her a little squeeze, she adds, "They'd have enjoyed tonight. Sitting around the table, listening in to everyone's stories, the kids teasing each other..."

"They're probably both busy up there unionising the angels and organising protest marches," offers Ignacio.

"Can angels march? I always see them as floating," wonders Guillermina.

"Protest floats doesn't really have that ring of action about it, does it?", murmurs Ignacio sleepily. The words curl and drift off with their thoughts.

Guillermina reflects yet again on that night when her husband drove off and the argument they'd had in this same room about him going to the meeting. They'd wrestled like the serpent spirits *Trentren Vilu* and *Caicai Vilu*, his land to her water as ever. Eventually, she'd given in. He was right. He had to go. That truth has eased her through the years since, yet still she wishes... She comes back to her son and lays her hands on his own. "Is this finally the one?"

Ignacio rocks his chin on her head.

"Good, get back to her soon then. You're not getting any younger yourself, you know." And with that she takes a handful of water and throws it up behind her.

Self-Reflection

1. How much do you feel you are your own person?
2. What about you is not wholly your own true self?
3. Is there anything you've ever been convinced you had to do whatever the consequences?
4. How did or would you describe this need to others?

17. The Tribe Share Their Learning

Henry lays a slim briefcase down in front of him and smiles. "No beanbags this time at least." He looks round their faces to gauge the mood. The scattering of Silvia's ashes into the sea this morning had been understandably emotional for all concerned. He's mindful of her wish for this meeting to be a celebration, yet he doesn't want to dishonour their memories of Silvia.

They're sitting in a small circle in the main gallery of the Huilliche *Inchin Cuivi Anti* museum in Quellón. The circle has expanded from last year to include Guillermina, Montse, and Harmony this time. Henry's sure Silvia would have approved.

The solicitor looks at his watch. "3pm, 26th February. Well done, all of you. Shall we begin?"

To their nods, he pulls out a sheet of paper. He checks to see they all have their cowbells beside them and smiles. Henry has always liked things to be done properly.

He starts. "A year ago, we gathered in Silvia's school in Edinburgh to hear the initial part of her last will and testament. In this, she set tasks for each of you to fulfil. Today, we are going to hear from each of you what your task was and what your learning over the last year has been. Are there any questions on this? No? Then I will turn to David first."

He looks at the young man sitting opposite him. "David, your sentence was, *I am rooted*. What was your task and what's been your learning?"

Taking his cue from the solicitor, David looks round his family watching him expectantly and smiles. He drops his eyes to the ground in the middle to focus. "My task was to bring Mum home and to find myself." He pauses for a moment. "By that, I first thought Mum meant I should find out about our history, where we come from, our Chilean and Huilliche heritage, all that. And she did. But then I realised she also meant my beliefs, what I stand for, what I value, and who and what has influenced me all the way up to who I am now. That's been my learning. That even as we look forward, we are everything that has gone before... I am rooted." He raises his eyes to his family's once more.

Without prompting, Ignacio spontaneously starts ringing his cowbell. One by one all join in until Harmony puts her hands over her ears to their laughter. David beams from ear to ear.

"And what's your way forward?", asks Henry as the peals of the bells die down.

David flicks his eyes to Montse and then back to the solicitor. "I'm going to finish my Master's in Spain and then, in time, I'll do a PhD. I'm interested in universal myths and rites across different cultures and how they vary. As our world gets smaller, our differences are becoming ever more important. I want to help celebrate these. I'm thinking there's a role for me in advocacy.... Probably through teaching and writing. Still working on the path, as you can see," he finishes off apologetically.

Sitting next to him, Kieran looks at his son and marvels at how he's grown over the last year. He thinks how enthused Silvia would have been by what David's just said. He can't stop himself resting a proud hand on his knee.

Henry waits for a second before turning his attention to Gabriella. "Your sentence was, *I am excellent*. Tell us about your year," he encourages gently.

Gabriella smiles at Harmony sitting on the floor in front of her, and then brings her eyes to the others'. "My task was to get into drama school and get great... Little did I know at the time, but the first part of that was the easier one. I thought the get great bit would come naturally... More fool I," she grins at the group. "So, what has my learning been? ... Unsurprisingly perhaps, that it takes hours and days and weeks and months and more of dedication and practice and sheer bloody hard work to get great at something. It's about honing skills and talents, constantly stretching yourself, pushing yourself out of your comfort zone, failing and falling and getting right back on the horse... And to do this, you need a real passion for what you do. A really pure passion where you're not thinking of money or fame or anything like that, but just of getting great. Doing something to the best of your ability. When I talk to David or *Abuela* about it, it's like a zen thing. Sorry, not very technical but I think you get what I mean..." She drifts off, lost in her thoughts, before adding, "And so endeth my monologue." Her eyes crinkle. "Oh yes, sorry. Space cadet... Way forward is complete drama school and..." She pauses dramatically. "I've got a part in a Harry Potter spinoff. We start shooting in the summer." She beams as the others cheer.

Down below her, Harmony reaches for her mother's gold-coloured cowbell and tries to give it a ring. The others laugh and all join in with their own. Harmony giggles as she's taken up into her mother's lap and hugged.

Henry turns his gaze to Kieran, who nods. "For me it was, *I am authentic*. And the task was to write a book. And to find my voice. Maybe not in that order." He grins and then his face falls serious. "The book... well, the first draft is done. Thank you," he says to their applause before continuing. "The book has been a big part of the learning. We all hear about writing something that reflects yourself, and that is very correct. For years I've tried different things, but when I thought of writing about depression, my depression, it immediately rang true. And so being true to myself has been to do what I really want to do, which is write, and also to face up to something that I've had for years and which has affected all my relationships." His voice grows huskier as he quickly glances from one to the other of his three children. "All my relationships," he repeats.

"And so yes, being true to yourself and others is about not pretending to be someone else, and about doing what you're meant to be doing. It's like your heart singing." He finishes and nods to himself more than to the group. "And my way forward is to publish this book and then to write another and then to write another. I'm also planning a meet-up group for guys to talk about depression, but I haven't fully worked out the details yet."

Mauricio is the first to start ringing his bell but he's soon drowned out in the noise of everyone else too. In the din, Kieran looks round at his family humbly. "Thanks. I love you all."

It takes a while for the room to settle. As it finally does, Jacqui speaks up for the first time. "Silvia knew how bad I am at all this so she gave me, *I am loose.*" The others laugh as she shakes herself and continues, "Yup, I had no idea what the crazy fool meant either... Until I read my task, which was, *Break free and jump.* Then it started to make some sense. Terrifying, white-knuckle, rollercoaster scary, but sense too if you know and love Silvia like we all do..."

Her voice stumbles and then comes back more quietly and also more powerfully. "My learning has been that much as we might think we want or need to change, we have to dig into ourselves and see how ready we are for it. We need to look at our lives – true to ourselves like this beautiful man just said - and see what we're prepared to give up. Because if we're going to go in one direction, we're saying no to a whole load of other directions. And when we're clear and we understand all this and we're ready to step forward, we have to find some way, some strength to take that first step. Because staying as we are will always be so much easier, even if it's the worst thing we could do..."

Catching Henry's eye, Jacqui goes on, "My first step was to take up some of Silvia's refugee work. But that was just a baby step. My real step was Médecins Sans Frontières. I've been in Nepal for a few months, got nearly a year to go. I've already decided I'm going to extend for another year. And then maybe Haiti. It would be good to be in the Caribbean again after all the cold." She smiles and before anyone else can get there, she picks up her little silver cowbell and looks up to the ceiling. "I am loose." She gives her bell a soft ring at the heavens above as the others chime in more fully.

"Wow. Wow wow wow. And now it's my turn," exclaims Ignacio, pulling a nervous face. "I... *I have a mission*. That was my sentence. And my task was to go and find the child who wanted to heal the world.... Is there anything that my big sister didn't know? I thought it was just me who got that I was bored." Catching the roll of eyes from his mother, he says, "OK, Mama, you knew. But you're a witch, it doesn't count."

Ignacio chuckles to himself and then continues more seriously. "I think I've always had a pretty cool mission. *Tikkun olam*. Heal the world. It's why I do what I do. But yes... I needed a new impetus, a new goal. Yet it took another woman to knock some sense into me. Literally. Off my bike literally. OK, yes, it's a terrible joke. I'll work on it... Lucía showed me a new mission. So...my learning is that our mission, our goals, call it what you will, our way forward can evolve. It doesn't have to be a life thing. It's a journey, and along the way other aspects will become important, maybe even take over. But it needs to be fresh and, most importantly, in the service of something bigger than yourself. Lucía's an amazing woman. Everything she does is in the service of others... And so my way forward is the foundation. I'll continue with my hands work too, but I'm shifting my practice to Santiago so I can be closer to this old bat," he says, nodding at his mother.

To their laughter, Guillermina throws her hands up in the air. "And I just finally got rid of David..."

"And... And I'm going to marry that Cubana if she's mad enough to have me." He settles back into his seat as if just fully comprehending that last sentence for the first time.

Montse leans towards him, "She'll be lucky to have you."
Ignacio does the closest a surgeon ever will to blushing as the cowbells roar around the hall.

Henry lets the noise subside and then swivels to Mauricio beside him. "And you, Mauricio? What have you learnt about *I have momentum*?"

Mauricio raises his gaze from the floor and examines them all one by one. "I see Nepal and Havana and Tarragona and Quellón, and I think maybe my story's a bit different... Mum gave me, *I have momentum*, and I thought, *Well duh, momentum's what I've always had. I'm a consultant. I'm always on the move...* And then I saw the task, which was..." And his voice falters. "*Surround yourself with love...*" He waits for some strength and holds three fingers up. "So, three things I've learnt..." He waves off their good-natured groans. "Three things. First is, I've always been surrounded by love..." And he can't help himself. The tears flow down his cheeks. Gabriella puts her arm around his shoulder and even Harmony looks upset.

Mauricio catches his niece's expression and says, "Don't worry, my darling. Your uncle's just a stupid man. You'll find there are plenty of us." He grins at her, and after a beat resumes. "I've always been surrounded by love, and I was just too self-absorbed and self-focussed to realise it."

He bends down a second finger. "Second is that however far I go or however great I get or whatever I do in fact, I will always need this love. I will always need someone to support me unconditionally or to hold me accountable to my promises or to tell it to me straight. To call me a dick when I'm being a dick. Or even coach or mentor me. Whatever it is I need. We don't get to where we want to go alone...

And the third thing is that I, we need to ask for this love as well. We have to recognise when we need it and be unashamed in asking for it. Sooner rather than later. And that's what keeps the momentum going."

Yet again Mauricio looks from one face to another. "My way forward is a small consultancy as I've mentioned to some of you. Something which doesn't involve travelling the world. I'll need your support getting it up and running... But Dad, the depression group idea, and Ignacio, with the foundation, and with you Jacqui, and Gabriella, and David... If there's anything I can do, just let me know... And yes, one more thing. I've been sober for 88 days. I'm also going to need your help staying this way."

It's not just Mauricio's cheeks that are wet as the cowbells peal out once more.

After a long, long time, one by one the group turn to look at Henry expectantly. He eyes his sheet of paper and then thinks better of it. "If I may...", he starts diffidently. "I hope I'm not presuming, but I think there's a piece missing. And I think Silvia, in her own remarkable way, was aware of this." He holds up the spare cowbell he took a year ago. "And so... We've had *I am rooted*, and *I am excellent*, and *I am authentic*, and then also *I am loose*. For me, these are all about exploring yourself and understanding who you are. The *real* you if you like. That's our foundation, our underland in a manner of speaking... Then there's *I have a mission* and *I have momentum*. These are the way forward, just like we've been discussing. But I think there's a third *m... I have a map*. We may know where we want to go, but we need a map, a clear guide to get there. It sounds obvious, but so often

I see people heading out into the wild without a plan. We may have a mission and momentum, but we also need to map out the steps and the milestones to show us how we're going to get there. The stone cairns that will guide us along our way... *I have a map.*"

Gabriella smiles at him. "*REALM.* Mum did like an acronym."

Still deep in his thoughts, Henry turns to her, "Yes, I can well believe that." He returns his attention to the wider group. "So that's perhaps the last element of the picture...REALM, as Gabriella put it... And yet, there's more. It only came to me just now listening to the wonderful things each one of you is doing, and also recalling something my daughter Josie said. Over the last year I've been wondering what Silvia meant with her emphasis on living well. She was so strong about it... I've always been a planner, just like my father was. And it's an important part of what we're all engaging in. Yet Josie's right, life twists and turns in ways that can be good and bad, blissful and downright awful. So... I hope I can phrase this correctly... I think it's not wholly about some bright peak on the horizon, some distant point in the future. This is our vision, our guiding star for sure, but in this mixture of elements – *I am rooted* and all else – the real crux of what we're achieving is that we're living well in the here and now. The destination is less important than the journey..."

Kieran, his eyes alight, interrupts. "*There's never anything but the present*, as the saying has it."

"Exactly." Henry looks round the circle to see how this lands. He nods to himself as if reassured before finishing off. "We live our best life in stretching and challenging ourselves, in growing and giving and all else that makes us full. I think Silvia was telling us to embrace this moment and dance in it like she did. Does that sound right to you?" Jacqui beams at him, "It does indeed. I think you'd make a good mountain mystic."

And they all laugh, Henry the loudest of anyone. As the laughter dies down, Jacqui continues, "So, Henry, you've asked us, let's ask you. What's your way forward?"

Henry seems taken aback at the question, but then smiles. "Well, this will be news to you, but this is my last official engagement for the Maclean legal practice. I'm retiring as of today." Seeing Ignacio's look of surprise, he quickly adds, "Don't worry, I'll continue my role with the trust. Pro bono as before of course... Yes, I'm retiring. Thank you, no need to cheer. I hope I wasn't that bad at it...! I've already moved up north to near Aviemore, and while I'm still fit and healthy, I'm going to finish off the Munros and help out with the mountain rescue teams. I'm sure Guillermina could manage it, but for this old man it may be more support from a desk than hauling someone off a cliff face on a stretcher, but we'll see. Whatever I can do."

And with this Henry breaks off to enjoy the cowbells in all their glory. He waits for a moment before picking up his piece of paper again and resuming. "Anyway, the final point to address is the financial side of Silvia's will... Having successfully accomplished your tasks, it was her wish that you would pool all of your individual entitlements and, with your unanimous approval, donate the lump sum to one or more charities or institutions of your choice. You don't need to make your decision today, but Guillermina has suggested that this building we are sitting in right now would be a fantastic way to honour Silvia and all she was and is."

Henry looks round their faces to see their reaction. With a huge grin, David holds his cowbell in front of him. *"Pura vida,"* he shouts and rings the bell loudly in agreement. The others laugh and one by one they all join in. The ringing of the cowbells roars through the halls of the museum of their ancestors.

And somewhere, wherever she is, Silvia smiles.

Self-Reflection

1. How much do you agree that there's nothing but the present?
2. Looking back, which of the characters most resonates with you?
3. What is it about them that talks to you?
4. What can you apply from their journey to your own?

Our REALM

The table below captures a summary of the **REALM** model we used to underpin the characters' exploration of themselves and their way forward. It's formed by the seven elements we touched on in the story towards mapping out a way forward and a full life.

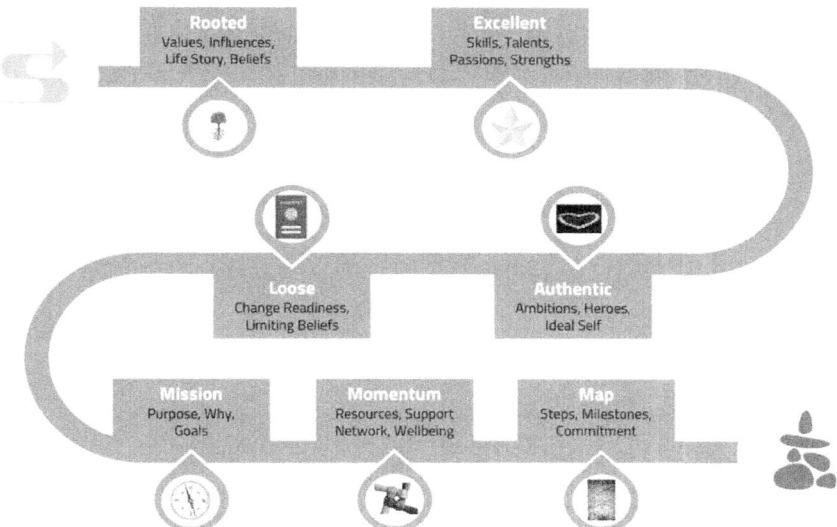

In brief, and as Henry summarises at the end in Quellón for us, the first four elements – **Rooted, Excellent, Authentic,** and **Loose** – concern our understanding and knowledge of ourselves. The latter three – **Mission, Momentum,** and **Map** – are our way forward. This will mean and be something different for all of us – our purpose, our meaning, our way of living fully, our *ikigai*, our reason for being here, our guiding star, our big hairy audacious goal, our ticket off the sofa, our call to get out of bed every morning...

It is only with the lucidity and clarity provided by exploring the **REAL** elements that we can lay the foundation for a successful and sustainable way forward. Many of us believe we have this self-awareness, when in reality the research shows otherwise. Too often we just see the tip of our own iceberg. The more we probe and dig into ourselves, the better our chances are for an aligned and authentic path, and indeed for living fully in the moment.

This too is an important message our story leads us to. As Alan Watts said, "There's never anything but the present." Silvia was keen for her loved ones to live well in the here and now. Through pursuing a purposeful path, we can all do this.

Let's explore the seven elements in a little more detail to see what constitutes this path.

I am Rooted talks to our values, our influences, our beliefs, our life story, and all that has made us who we are today. It can seem strange to look back when we are thinking of a way forward. Yet understanding and embracing everything in our rear-view mirror – good and bad – clarifies our current Ground Zero.

I am Excellent concerns our skills, our talents, our passions, and our strengths. This is an element which can be more fully fleshed out by those who know us well. We may be surprised at the skills and strengths unknown to us which others see.

I am Authentic relates to being true to ourselves and to others. As such, it touches on ambitions, our heroes, and our ideal self. This can be a tough one to explore, for we may not like what we see.

I am Loose is about our limiting beliefs as well as our attitude and readiness to change. It looks at status quo and what we may need to give up to achieve what we desire. Loose as in an athlete, fit and limber, muscles warm and ready.

I have a Mission is the heart of our way forward, the bigger than us contribution we are looking to make. Simon Sinek would call this *our why*. For Michael Bungay Stanier it's *our worthy goal*. It's the direction of our way forward.

I have Momentum is everything we need to keep our engine oiled and ticking over as we work on our mission. Our support network, the props and people around us who will hold us true to and support to ensure we keep going. The resources we'll need for this, be it systems, funds, people, whatever. Most importantly perhaps, it also includes our own wellbeing and the need to care for ourselves.

I have a Map is Henry's area - our guide to the steps and milestones of how we're going to achieve what we're setting out to do, and also our commitment to our way forward.

If you're interested in learning more about the model and the various elements in more depth, please check out orangecairns.com. You'll find programmes, Postcards, and a whole host of free resources and activities which can help you explore your self-awareness, purpose, and a way forward.

Life's good. It's worth living well.

About The Author

Endlessly curious about the world, Julian is a full-time leadership and purpose coach who has partnered thousands of people in their development journey – be they starting out or drawing towards their destination. To this end, he recently founded orangecairns Ltd as a home base in Edinburgh for this exploration, despite being a child of the Caribbean.

Aside from living, travelling, and working in a variety of roles and sectors around the globe, he's also a writer and a slightly wistful poet. While Edinburgh gives him the Highlands and all things green, he's equally happy in the desert or underwater or in Tokyo's neon. A deep believer in untapped potential everywhere, he fully expects to climb the Inaccessible Pinnacle on Skye one day.

Gratitude

There are too many people to thank here in the journey of this book. No, there are never too many people to thank. There are so many to thank. Let's highlight the big names for this book in particular, yet the unmentioned others are also in my heart.

You, for picking this up and giving some of your precious time to it. From the bottom of my soul, I hope it has talked to you on some level. If you wish to follow up for more, there's a host of resources, programmes, and more at orangecairns.com. Please also leave a review with Amazon, refer the book to those who might appreciate it, and generally carry on being a wonderful person. You might even enjoy the forthcoming books in this series...

Adrian, Gavin, Leyan, Nicolai, and Sean for their generous and humbling pre-release reviews.

All my first readers – Ali, Beverley, Ferdinand, Judy, Julia, Loren, Merry – for doing what is a painful and tortuous task – reading something in draft and then deliberating on just how to frame the feedback as softly as possible.

Adrian, David, Elliot, Gabriel, Jesús, Lee, Nicky (thanks for the title!), and Marily (thanks for the cover!) for the constant friendship and challenge. If you need a website or a designer or just an amazing force of inspiration, Marily is your person.

All my brilliant coachees, mentors, coaches, and anyone who's shared their life with me in some format or other. Your stories have blended and fused into the REALM model and into this.

My beautiful mother, my beautiful sister and her equally beautiful children, to who this book is dedicated.

And to my very first and last reader, Pascale, for everything. Truly everything.

A percentage of any profits will go to the Samaritans and to Scottish Mountain Rescue, two causes close to my heart.

Thank you and be well.

Printed in Great Britain
by Amazon

15648920R10098